Praise for Steven Leech

As a radio host and producer
"[S]ince 1984, Steven [Leech] has distinguished himself as a well-rounded source of entertainment and information for WVUD listeners. . . . His ability to provide background information and a historical context for the selections that he chooses is unmatched. His knack for connecting much of this music to our local community is also noteworthy."
—Steven Leech's WVUD Wall of Fame proclamation.

As novelist
"Behold this letter to God [*Raw Suck*] misdelivered to the reader. Leech is an idealist offering Hell not as it is, but as he dreams it into being."
—Douglas Morea, poet

And generally
"Steven Leech is Delaware's preeminent person of letters."
—Phillip Bannowsky, educator and poet

Also by Steven Leech

Novels
The Afternoon Detective Agency
Powmia Among the Dragonflies
Poe's Daughter, Pym's Soul
2000 Years
Raw Suck
Untime
Jobe In Exile
Goomplotz

Short Fiction
The Secret Life of Tux Munce
Breath and Glamour
The Last Place on Earth

Non-fiction
The Wedgehorn Manifesto
A City of Ghosts
Valdemar's Corpse

Boysie's Horn

Boysie's Horn
The History of Jazz in Wilmington in the Twentieth Century

Steven Leech

Boysie's Horn: The History of Jazz in Wilmington in the 20th Century

Copyright©2022 by Steven Leech

All rights reserved. No part of this publication may be reproduced, distributed, or transmitted in any form by any means, or stored in a database or retrieval system, without the prior written permission of the author, except in the case of brief quotations embodied in critical articles and reviews.

❦ BROKEN TURTLE BOOKS ❦
Newark, Delaware

ISBN: 0-97809788451-6-2

Library of Congress Control Number: 2021948371

First Broken Turtle Books Edition February 2022

Author photo in Bio by Nina Leech

Contents

Introduction 1
One: A Syncopating City of Lost Music 4
Two: Little Comache 11
Three: Jazz Daredevil 22
Four: Bop Cop in Brown's Town 29
Illustrations 39
Five: Jes Grew, Jim Crow,
    and the Wrecking Ball 60
Six: The Day Junie Left Town 73
Seven: From Boysie's Basement
    to The Flight Deck 80
Afterward by Larry Williams 87
Index 93
Author's Bio 105

INTRODUCTION

I'd like to acknowledge the work, knowledge, and goodwill of those who contributed to what follows. First is Scott Davidson, who, before his passing in 2020, had intended to write a book about Wilmington jazz artist Lem Winchester. As a result, through the goodwill of Davidson's widow Rebecca L. Fisher, I was bequeathed his research materials, which I have subsequently donated to the University of Delaware Library's Special Collections. Scott's collection is largely the reason why the heart of this short tome centers on Lem Winchester.

The story of jazz in Wilmington after that fateful day in June 1956 begins with Lem Winchester and his short career in the jazz limelight. Unlike the equally short career of his predecessor Clifford Brown, Lem Winchester remained a working resident of the city, walking the beat as a Wilmington police officer.

I also need to acknowledge Maurice Sims, a friend for more than forty years. Maurice was also very good friends with Lem Winchester during their years growing up together in Wilmington. It is from Maurice that some insight into the nature of Lem's earliest years comes. Maurice, now in his mid-90s, was also able to provide the names of many of those in the old historic photos accompanying the text.

Contributions by Bob Fleming, Dimitri Kogomahalis, and Ken Anderson also played a significant role in completing this story of jazz in Wilmington, and even though Ken and Dimitri are no longer with us, their contributions need to be acknowledged.

Hats off as well to the Delaware Historical Society for providing some of those historic photos.

I wish to dedicate this work not only to my dear friend Maurice Sims but to the memory of Ralph Morris, the youngest brother of Henry "Peck" Morris, who formed one of the earliest jazz bands in Wilmington, "The Radio Boys." My earliest association with Ralph was as a journalist with *The Delaware Spectator,* a Wilmington monthly newspaper that Ralph published, later leading him to earn the moniker of "The Dean of Delaware Black Journalism." Ralph, an accomplished musician, was also a close friend and neighbor of Clifford Brown. In my endeavors as a member of the local Black press—*The Delaware Spectator*, *The Delaware Star*, *The Wilmington Gazette,* and *The Wilmington Spectator*—I need to thank not only Ralph Morris but also successive editors of those newspapers, including Herman Holloway, Jr., Felix Stickney, and Vaughn Morris, Ralph's son, for believing in me, which allowed me to soak in the rich and remarkable history of Wilmington's Black community.

Finally, but by no means least, I want to thank my old friend Phillip Bannowsky for devoting many hours to make this short book a more attractive product with text editing, constructing its index, and improving the graphics in order to enhance its visual content. And importantly, I want to acknowledge those from whom I've derived much inspiration and support over the years. Besides Vaughn Morris, and members of the entire Morris family, also Michael "Mafundi" Kennard, Patrice Gibbs, Mitch Thomas, and Larry Williams—in his own right a superb musician and dedicated historian of the unique American classical music called jazz. To all those named here, I appreciate you more than you may know.

Chapter One
A Syncopating City of Lost Music

At the turn of the 20th century, Wilmington was a quiet city where two industrial monoliths, the duPonts and the Bancrofts, made the economy hum, kept Jim Crow order, and set the cultural tone. The east side of Wilmington was filling up with African Americans, largely from the great Southern migration, who, along with many established families, would live out their lives there. People in other parts of the city, many from different sorts of early 20th century migrations and those generations already there for decades, were mostly oblivious to what was flourishing on the city's east side.

On the Eastside, Alice Dunbar, recently separated from the great American poet Paul

Laurence Dunbar, spread her literary influence and social and cultural sensibilities to nurture a community. The Redding brothers, Louis L. and J. Saunders, soon followed, and others who believed in the potential of a unique community fell into their contributing roles.

As years progressed, institutions like Howard High School and the Walnut Street YMCA played a crucial part in developing a vibrant community.

During those post-World War I years, the Spanish flu epidemic hit Wilmington especially hard, almost as if mocking the birthing pains that issued forth a renaissance child. Reflecting a new era spilling over from the Harlem Renaissance, Wilmington was quietly experiencing a nearly parallel renaissance, manifested through the medium of music.

In those post-World War I years, Paul F. Thompson's Dixieland Jazz Band awoke in the eardrums of local music fans. Thompson's band was an integrated ensemble that included Clarence Sheppard, who later reportedly performed with renowned early blues and jazz singer Mamie Smith, Jessie McCoy Hanson, who played the bass mandolin, and Willard Burns Chippey, who was not only the long-standing organist at Wilmington's Mother African Union Church, but he also played an instrument of his own invention in the Paul F. Thompson Dixieland Band. That instrument was called a "violbone," a cross between string and a brass instrument.

In the 1920s, a couple of other local jazz bands emerged in Wilmington. Henry "Peck" Morris was born on September 10th, 1901. As a teenager, he worked as a tailor at Caney's Tailor Shop on 7th Street in Wilmington before attending Howard University. He studied the trumpet to become a member of the Howard University band. Returning to Wilmington, he joined the Radio Boys and became the band's leader, later dubbing it Peck & the Radio Boys. Another was the Claude and Artie Wells Band, from which sprang many of Wilmington's top-shelf musicians in ensuing decades.

Most of the streets in Wilmington during the 1920s were paved with brick or Belgium block. A few in the oldest parts of the city were still paved with cobblestone, like Lord, Curlett, and Klund Streets in the lower southeast corner of the Eastside. Small, nearly impromptu speakeasies sprung up in Prohibition-strapped Wilmington. Daisy Winchester's fun time house was on Klund Street while Dollar Bill's Grotto on McCauly Alley sat under the shadow of the Allied Kidd tannery on East 12th Street, as depicted in the short story "Delaware Coon," written by J. Saunders Redding. Perhaps the most notable speakeasy was Daisy Winchester's fun time house. Her fame spread to the radio, where for a time she had a back-to-back spot with Crash Peyton. Peyton graduated Friends School, was the city's answer to Bing Crosby, and wrote science fiction published in *Amazing Stories* magazine. Daisy sang live at any number of legitimate venues springing up on the Eastside, as well, mostly with Boysie and Bud Lowery's Deuces of Rhythm and Jimmy Hinsley & His Maniacs of Rhythm. In 1940, Daisy would make the first commercial recording by a Wilmington artist: "You've Got To Go When The Wagon Comes," with up-and-coming Louis Jordan and his Tympany Five. Daisy was followed a year later by another Wilmington native from the Eastside, Betty Roché, singing "At's In There" with the Savoy Sultans.

Having grown up on East 12th Street, Betty Roché's family moved from Wilmington to Atlantic City when she was a teenager. Then she headed to New York City when she was old enough, eventually hooking up with Duke Ellington's band in the early 1940s. She appeared on film with the Ellington band in the movie *Reveille With Beverly* in 1943, singing "Take the 'A' Train." She also performed live with Ellington at Carnegie Hall and had a singing role in Ellington's *Black, Brown & Beige Suite* on January

23rd of the same year.

The Eastside of Wilmington became a vibrant and thriving town throughout the 1930s despite the Great Depression that plagued the country. Small Black-owned businesses sprang up throughout the neighborhood: barbershops like Burton's Tonsorial Parlor, gas stations like the King Street Service Center at 818 King Street, beauty parlors like Na's Beauty Shoppe at 429 East 11th Street, and eateries like Miss Elsie's Chicken Shack at 1200 Walnut Street and Thomas Reeder's Restaurant at 11th and Walnut. Levin Waters Confectionery sold ice cream, cigars, and cigarettes at 328 East 7th Street, Samuel's Dry Goods store operated at 318 East 11th Street, and the National Theater stood at 820 French Street. On the second floor of the National was the home of the *Wilmington Herald Times*, a broadsheet newspaper that was published twice a week and included a sports page and a society page, among other features, in addition to the latest news from Wilmington's Black community. During the Second World War, the *Herald Times* was absorbed into the *Philadelphia Tribune*, still in print.

In addition to the Club Harlem at 9th and Poplar Streets, other venues that made the town jump were the Spot Grille at 703 French Street, the Circle Bar at 8th and Poplar, Bill's Café at 312 East 8th Street, and others like George's Café and the Palace Café. Besides Peck Morris's band, there was the Claude & Artie Wells band, which featured tenor saxophonist Coleman Allen, who continued to perform locally into the 1970s. Other bands were the Deuces of Rhythm, Joe Thomas and His Royal Swingsters, Jimmy Hinsley and His Maniacs of Rhythm, and bands led by Felix Brown, Wilber Seal, and Chick Smith, who lent his services as an arranger for many of the aforementioned ensembles.

When the United States' involvement in World War II came along, cultural activity on the Eastside, as everywhere else, took a pause until the late 1940s.

After the War, Wilmington's Club Harlem became the Club Baby Grand, but Wilmington, one of America's wellsprings of jazz, would not achieve the same notice as places like Kansas City or New Orleans. Except for that one recording by Daisy Winchester in 1940 with Louis Jordan's Tympany 5, or even that one recording by Betty Roché with the Savoy Sultans in 1941, the jazz artists from Wilmington were never commercially recorded, except by local radio stations WDEL and WILM.

Those recordings were recorded for single plays on a later broadcast, would not hold up for successive turns under the needle, and were eventually consigned to the garbage heap. No one seemed to realize the importance of their legacy for later generations who would want to hear, save, and cherish them. While we can still hear, for example, the music of Jay McShann, the band from Kansas City that spawned Charlie Parker, or that of Cab Calloway, or Fletcher Henderson, or Andy Kirk and his 12 Clouds of Joy, or even lesser-known bands of the 1930s like Cecil Scott and His Bright Boys, or Willie Bryant and His Orchestra, or Boots and His Buddies, we will never hear the Wilmington jazz bands of the late 1920s and 30s. We will never hear Peck Morris' Radio Boys. They've been trashed. We will never hear the Claude and Artie Wells Band. They've been trashed. We will never hear the Deuces of Rhythm. They have all been trashed, along with early recordings of Daisy Winchester, Queen Belle, and Crash Peyton, among others.

As my friend Maurice Sims—Delaware's second Black radio disc jockey after Mitch Thomas and the first to broadcast Clifford Brown's inaugural commercial recording in 1952—declared, "There are three cities jazz came from: New Orleans, Kansas City, and Wilmington, Delaware. New York and Chicago are where jazz went."

Chapter Two
Little Comache

On October 30th, 1930, while jazz was beginning to build a head of steam in Wilmington, a boy was born who would blow the top off that world of jazz. That boy was Clifford Brown, the final child among seven other siblings. Born into a working-class family of music lovers in Wilmington's Eastside, young Clifford, or "Little Comache," as his young peers would call him, was drawn to that shiny horn his father had in his collection of musical instruments. As young Clifford grew up among the accomplished musicians living only blocks away, some on his own block on Poplar Street, Little Comache grew more proficient as a young musician. By the time he entered Howard High School in

1944, he was good enough to join the Howard High School marching band.

One fortunate event that occurred during his years with his high school band was the new music teacher hired by Howard High. His name was Sam Wooding.

Wooding had already enjoyed a very successful professional career. Born in nearby Philadelphia on June 17th, 1895, Wooding formed a band in New City in the 1920s, during the blossoming of the Jazz Age in the United States and the dawning of The Harlem Renaissance. Instead of remaining in New York, Wooding took his band, The Chocolate Dandies, to Europe, where they performed widely throughout the continent and recorded on a number of labels like Pathé, Parlophone, and Polydor. Perhaps like no one else, Wooding brought the uniquely American art form of jazz to Europeans, influencing composers like Darius Milhaud and Kurt Weill with this exciting new music.

By the mid-1930s, the scourge of Nazism began to change the cultural climate in Europe, and to make a long story short, Wooding and his band had to return to the United States, where the Great Depression made it difficult for what seemed like an emerging new jazz band to gain traction. As a result, Wooding returned to school and got a Masters' Degree from the University of Pennsylvania, which got him his teaching position at Howard High School during World War II, when Clifford Brown was a student. Working alongside music teacher Harry Andrews, Sam Wooding was probably Clifford Brown's earliest music teacher and mentor.

Soon after Clifford graduated from Howard in 1948, or perhaps during his school years, he began taking lessons from the legendary Robert "Boysie" Lowery. During one of those lessons, which Boysie conducted in the basement of his house on nearby Pine Street, Clifford's first recording was made: Charlie Parker's "Ornithology," with Boysie leading on saxophone and Clifford playing right along on trumpet. In fact, the recording may be the only recording of Boysie playing music.

As mentioned in the previous chapter, Boysie Lowery was a prime member of the Deuces of Rhythm band. Boysie became a teacher and mentor of nearly all budding musicians aiming to gain success and keep Wilmington a cookin' town for the next quarter-century.

After World War II had ended and Brown was leaving Howard High School, he formed his own combo, with Donald Criss (later Rashid Yaya) on piano and Bobby Burton on bass. The trio was joined by returning war veteran Bob Cordrey on tenor sax and—possibly—Red

Clyde on drums. The effort allowed Brown to find his own voice and sharpen his chops with the help of neighbor Ralph Morris. Morris was the youngest brother of Henry "Peck" Morris and was also a returning veteran, and he later joined Cordrey's combo after Clifford went away to Delaware State College.

From the excellent film *Brownie Speaks*, produced by local musician and teacher Don Glanden, and the biography *Clifford Brown, The Life and Art of the Legendary Jazz Trumpeter* by Nick Catalano, we learn that Clifford attended Delaware State College and the University of Maryland, during which time he suffered a near fatal automobile accident. In the course of his long convalescence at home, he continued to sharpen his skills, even learning to play the piano and taking lessons from Boysie Lowery.

As we read in Glanden and Catalano's works cited above, as well from as my own article, "A Found Cacophony" (*DREAMSTREETS #58* Summer 2018, Newark, Delaware), young Clifford's abilities first found notice when Dizzy Gillespie allowed him to sit in with him during a performance at Wilmington's Odd Fellows Temple at 12th and Orange Street. The cat was out of the bag when Dizzy heard Brownie play. The event led to any number of engagements throughout the area, including Philadelphia.

Among the earliest was a gig in Philadelphia in 1951 at the Club Harlem with bebop great Charlie Parker. It's been reported that Parker told Clifford in response to the young 21-year old's performance, "I don't believe it. I hear what you're saying, but I don't believe it."

Those sessions of Charlie Parker and Clifford Brown were never recorded, adding to the list of music performed by Wilmington jazz artists that will never be heard.

Another of Clifford's earliest gigs was at Philadelphia's Pep Bar, where he played with Jimmy Heath on alto sax, Charlie Coker at the piano, Bob Berton on bass, and Joe Jane on drums. That engagement led to Clifford's hire by Chris Powell and his Blue Flames, with whom Brownie made his first commercial recording, "Ida Red," inspired by his girlfriend at the time Ida Mae Wade, followed by "I Come From Jamaica."

In 1953, Clifford left Chris Powell, a largely R&B act, and turned to jazz. Word had got out about the phenom from Wilmington, and the whirlwind began.

Later that year, Clifford joined a recording session on June 9th with alto sax musician Lou Donaldson, with Elmo Hope on piano, Percy Heath on bass, and Philly Joe Jones on drums. Two days later, he recorded a session with Tadd

Dameron's Big Ten. This included Dameron on piano, Idress Sulieman on trumpet, Herb Mullins on trombone, Gigi Gryce on alto, Benny Golson on tenor sax, Oscar Estell on baritone sax, Percy Heath on bass, and Philly Joe Jones on drums. Those sessions led to Clifford Brown being hired by Lionel Hampton for a European tour in late 1953.

By the end of the Korean War, Clifford Brown would begin to wow jazz musicians on the European continent. Because Hampton strictly forbad any gigs outside his band during this tour, a number of his musicians would sneak away to surreptitiously perform with some top-shelf European jazz musicians known as the Swedish All Stars in Stockholm. With arrangements by Quincy Jones, the All Stars included an array of Swedish musicians and American trumpet player Art Farmer.

Later in September, Brownie was in Paris again with compatriots Art Farmer, Quincy Jones, trumpeter Walter Williams, and sax man Gigi Gryce. Joined by eminent French jazz cats Henri Renaud on piano, Pierre Michelot on bass, Jean-Louis Viale on drums, and others, Brownie recorded more than a dozen tunes in all.

After sharpening his chops with many of the big names in international and domestic jazz, Brownie returned to the United States in late 1953. On February 21st, 1954, he got a gig at the famed Birdland in New York City with Art Blakey, the jazz drummer who would launch the Jazz Messengers. Playing with Brownie and Blakey were alto saxophonist Lou Donaldson, Horace Silver on piano, and Curly Russell on bass. The recording, issued on the Blue Note label, as had been many of the previously mentioned recordings, is arguably the most torrid, accomplished recording that Brownie ever made, including a stunningly beautiful rendition of the standard "Once In A While."

Also early in 1954, at the urging of some of his jazz peers, Brownie ventured to Los Angeles to Eric Dolphy's house to meet and jam with some west coast jazz cats and to form a regular unit with which he would tour and record. It was there that he met tenor saxophonist Harold Land, bassist George Morrow, Bud Powell's brother and pianist Richie Powell, and drummer Max Roach, in addition to pianist Carl Perkins and saxophonist Teddy Edward. During his sojourn in L. A., Clifford recorded an album on the Pacific Jazz label with Zoot Sims, baritone sax player Bob Gordon, trombonist Stu Williamson, Russ Freeman on piano, Joe Mondragon and Carson Smith alternating on bass, and Shelley Mann on drums. The album featured four of Brownie's own compositions.

The first configuration of the Clifford Brown/Max Roach Quintet included Carl Perkins on piano and Teddy Edwards on sax, later settling on Richie Powell on piano and Harold Land on sax. All, however, with George Bledsoe on bass, were featured on the ensemble's first live recording, *The Best of Max Roach and Clifford Brown in Concert* on the GNP Crescendo label in April 1954.

Signing with the EmArcy label, the Quintet's final ensemble comprised Clifford Brown, Max Roach, Harold Land, Richie Powell, and George Morrow and issued *Brown and Roach, Incorporated,* recorded in August 1954. The same month, on the 14th, the Quintet recorded a jam session with Dinah Washington, augmented with trumpet players Clark Terry and Maynard Ferguson, alto saxophonist Herb Geller, Junior Mance on piano, and Ketter Betts on bass,

Before heading east, Brown recorded an album with Sarah Vaughan on December 16th and 18th on the Verve label with musicians Herbie Mann on flute, Paul Quinichette on tenor sax, Jimmy Jones on piano, Joe Benjamin on bass, and Roy Haynes on drums. That album was followed by one recorded with singer Helen Merrill December 22nd through 24th on EmArcy with musician Danny Banks on various reeds and flute, Jimmy Jones on piano, Barry Galbraith on guitar, Milt Hinton and Oscar Pettiford on bass, and Osie Johnson and Bobby Donaldson on drums. The ensemble was arranged and conducted by Quincy Jones.

Among the Quintet's first live gigs was one at the Storyville Club in Boston in the spring of 1955. In January, the Quintet recorded *Clifford Brown with Strings*—a nuptial gift to his new wife LaRue—with the addition of Barry Galbraith on guitar and a string section arranged and conducted by Neal Hefti. The music comprised an array of ballads, including "Portrait of Jenny," "Stardust," and "Willow Weep for Me." In February, the Quintet had recorded the album *Study in Brown*, which contained four of Clifford's compositions, one by Richie Powell and one by Harold Land.

In April and May of 1955, the Quintet played an engagement at the Basin Street in New York City with a concert at Carnegie Hall on May 6th.

Finally returning home to Wilmington and the Philadelphia area, Brownie performed an afternoon gig at Music City in Philadelphia on May 31st. He was accompanied by Ziggy Vines and Billy Root on the tenor sax, Sam Dockery on piano, Ace Tisone on bass, and Ellis Tollin on drums, all Philly musicians.

After a quick breather at home in Wilmington, where the Quintet may have performed a gig for hometown fans at the Club Baby Grand, Max, Brownie, and the others hit the road again. They had an engagement at the Beehive in Chicago on June 30th, then the Newport Jazz Festival on July 16th, where Brownie jammed with Dave Brubeck, Chet Baker, Gerry Mulligan and other jazz notables, followed by an engagement in Quebec, Canada, on July 28th. After another gig at the Beehive in November, the Quintet headed back into the recording studio in January, February, and March of 1956 with jazz tenor saxophone great Sonny Rollins replacing Harold Land. The result would be two new albums: *Clifford Brown and Max Roach at Basin Street* and *Sonny Rollins Plus Four*.

The Quintet hit the road again. From May 28th to June 1st, 1956, they played the Cotton Club in Cleveland, Ohio. On June 18th, they performed at the Continental Restaurant in Norfolk, Virginia, broadcast on radio station WIOR.

A little more than a week later. Clifford Brown was back in Wilmington to visit with family and friends. Max Roach and Sonny Rollins had gone to Rudy Van Gelder's recording studio in Hackensack, New Jersey to record an album with pianist Tommy Flanagan and bassist Doug Watkins. That album would turn out to be Rollins' *Saxophone Colossus*. Afterwards, the five would rendezvous in Chicago for a live gig.

In the meantime, Brownie, pianist Richie Powell, and Powell's young wife Nancy met up in Wilmington, piled into Powell's new Pontiac, and headed for Chicago. It was Brownie's wife LaRue's birthday as well as their wedding anniversary. The date was June 26th, 1956.

Chapter Three

Jazz Daredevil

Lem Winchester could wiggle his ears. He'd press his face up against a window, making it broad and distorted, then wiggle his ears. It never failed to elicit a belly laugh. Lem always got a reaction, especially if it resulted in laughing or a small jolt of fear.

Lemuel Winchester's life as a jazz vibraphonist would end—like his predecessor Clifford Brown's— woefully too soon.

Life began for Lemuel Sewell Davis at Mercy Hospital in Philadelphia, where he was born to Marion Davis on March 19th, 1928. As a youngster, he was known as Ardell Davis.

The Davis family was a large family. Early in his life, young Lem was adopted by the

Honorable William J. Winchester, Delaware's first Black in the State legislature, and his wife Bessie. When he was old enough, he attended the Elbert School in the Southbridge section of Wilmington. An early and lifelong friend was Maurice Sims, who was a little more than a year older. It is from Maurice that much of Lem's early years in this recounting comes.

After grade school, Lem entered Howard High School. He played in the high school band during some of the same years as Clifford Brown and at the same time Sam Wooding was the band teacher. Lem's first choice of musical instrument was the piccolo. Later he chose the flute, then the saxophone, becoming proficient in all the instruments he chose to play.

Maurice tells the story about how Lem visited Sauter's Music Store on Wilmington's west side and bought an ocarina, a musical instrument also called a "potato." On the long walk to Lem's home in Southbridge, all through Wilmington's Eastside in between, Lem was learning the instrument, and by the time the pair got to Lem's house, he was proficient enough on the "potato" to toot out some complete tunes.

Lem Winchester graduated from Howard High School in 1944, excelling in history, math, English, French, and music. On his Wilmington Police application form in December 1949, he listed Jane Austin's *Pride and Prejudice* and Richard Wright's *Native Son* as his favorite books. In August 1945, he joined the Merchant Marines and, between calls to ship out, he worked as a truck driver and did odd jobs at J & S Market on North Scott Street and Austin O. Caulk on Pine Street. Between the summer of 1947 and 1948, he worked at PK Motors at 2102 Governor Printz Boulevard as a "lubricator," and left to play music. Before applying to the Wilmington Police Department in 1949, he was working for Hearn Brothers in Elsmere as a "produce man." When applying for work with the Wilmington Police Department, Lem gave as reasons, "The want of security for me and my family." There's also good reason to believe that his adopted father, William J. Winchester, who at the time was Superintendent for Wilmington's trash collectors, provided encouragement and exerted some influence with the city.

"Lem Winchester was the smartest man I ever knew," declared Maurice Sims.

Sometime after leaving the Merchant Marines, where he learned to box, Lem began to learn to play the vibraphone after experimenting on the grand piano at Howard High School with the one-finger method or style of piano playing popularized by Lionel Hampton.

"We'd climb through Pres Johnson's window on Buttonwood Street," reported Sims, "so that Lem could practice on his vibes."

Preston Johnson was a popular Wilmington jazz pianist who not only played with Lem Winchester but also performed at several post-war venues in Wilmington, including the Sans Souci and the Café Continental. He also accompanied singer Sharon Moore at New York's Apollo Theater and played behind Millie Cannon, Lem Winchester's sister and popular Wilmington jazz singer.

Lem Winchester joined the Wilmington Police Department after signing a loyalty oath on June 16th, 1950, only ten days before the outbreak of the Korean War.

There are similarities and differences between the musical aspirations of Clifford Brown and Lem Winchester. Both were members of the Howard High School band when Sam Wooding was the band teacher. Both were multi-instrumentalists. Clifford could not only play the trombone, but he later became an accomplished piano player. However, despite both having intellectual prowess, they followed different paths after high school. Clifford Brown continued his education by first going to Delaware State College and afterward the University of Maryland. Lem Winchester, instead, became a workingman, though both considered music their main endeavor. Both had close calls with the grim reaper. Clifford Brown was involved in a near-fatal automobile accident that required a lengthy recovery. Lem, at times, tempted fate with the grim reaper. In his application to the Wilmington Police Department, he stated that one of his hobbies was collecting guns. A flaw in his knowledge of them would prove fatal.

A story Maurice Sims tells about Lem demonstrates his daredevil inclinations. One day at Ellegood's Garage and Trucking at 5th and Lombard Street, several young motorcyclists were hanging out, guys with curious nicknames like "Boot Stockings," "Shotgun," and "Skinny." That last one, by the way, retained his nickname and later became Arthur "Skinny" Wilson, President of Longshoreman Local 1426 in Wilmington. Skinny Wilson worked for Ellegood, driving a truck and hauling coal. On that day when Lem and Maurice visited Ellegood's garage, Lem was gifted a yellow Harley Davidson motorcycle on condition that he could ride it. It may have been a dare, but who would want a yellow motorcycle? Even though Lem didn't know how to ride a motorcycle, the gift was too tempting. Lem took the motorcycle over to a vacant lot on Buttonwood Street, presumably after getting a quick briefing on how to go through the gears, how to hop on the startle peddle, and how to work the throttle to bring it roaring to life. He drove that bike around that vacant lot until he was confident enough to take it out onto the street.

"Hop on Ricie," Lem said, and Maurice did. Lem steered that yellow hog out to Concord Pike and sped out to Jimmy Johns up toward the Pennsylvania State line, a traditional hangout for motorcyclists in those days. A daredevil for speed, Lem cranked the throttle, with Maurice hanging on against increasing velocity and with Lem's cheeks rippling against the ripping wind. They tore both ways in the same fashion.

Lem Winchester knew something about guns. As already mentioned, he stated on his police application that he collected guns. He had once been charged with discharging a weapon within city limits, but the charge was dropped.

Regarding guns, Lem developed a trick using his standard police model Colt .38 to scare friends. I've encountered two variants of the trick, both closely related. The first variant is that he would take all the rounds out of the cylinder of the revolver and place one of them back into its chamber, which was the classic setup for Russian roulette. The other version was a scarier one in that he'd replace all the rounds in their chambers except one, thus leaving one chamber empty. After prepositioning the empty chamber under the pistol's firing pin, he'd spin the cylinder and by counting the clicks in the cylinder's ratchet, he could determine where the empty chamber was or where the live round was, depending on which version of the trick was used. Once he knew with confidence where the empty chamber or the live round was and that the firing pin would not hit a live round, he could point the gun at his head and squeeze the trigger, which would harmlessly go "click."

The only person I knew who witnessed the trick was Mitch Thomas, Delaware's first Black radio disc jockey.

"I saw him do it down at WILM," Mitch told me. "It was the scariest damn thing I ever saw. It scared the holy shit out of me."

On the other hand, Marian Allen, the proprietor of the Sans Souci Club in Wilmington, in a taped interview told late local musician and Lem Winchester researcher Scott Davidson that she'd seen Winchester perform the trick often in her apartment above her club. She was never frightened because she was confidant Lem was in full control and knew what he was doing.

Chapter Four
Bop Cop in Brown's Town

June 26th, 1956, was a traumatic day for Wilmington. Some reported that you could hear people sobbing on the block where Clifford Brown had lived. The sudden loss of Clifford Brown, then only 25 years old, along with Bud Powell's brother Richie, shocked the jazz world and drove those who knew and loved Brownie into deep disbelief and profound sorrow. In time, the house where he had lived died also. It's the only house in the ten hundred block of Poplar Street, now Clifford Brown Walk, that's no longer there.

Two events mitigated the grief felt across the community. On August 4th, jazz organist

Jimmy Smith gave a rip-roaring concert at the Club Baby Grand, recorded by Blue Note and opened with an introduction by radio personality Mitch Thomas.

Barely noticed was the release on the Bethlehem label of Wilmington native Betty Roché's first solo album. Among the major producers at Bethlehem, one had local connections. His name was James "Red" Clyde, and he had played drums for a jazz combo in Wilmington formed by Bob Cordrey. On trumpet was Ralph Morris, youngest brother of Henry "Peck" Morris, leader of the local Radio Boys from the 1930s. Others in the group were Preston Johnson on piano and George Haslan on bass. Red Clyde may also have played drums in Clifford Brown's very first band with Donald Criss and Bobby Burton. Red Clyde eventually left Wilmington and was among the founders of the Bethlehem label, serving as A&R man and later as a producer. One wonders if Red Clyde had anything to do with Betty Roché recording on the label or if it was a mere coincidence.

Bob Cordrey was a World War II veteran, served in the Marine Corps, and was a member of a Marine Corp band, which he credited with keeping him alive. After the War, he began frequenting the Circle Bar, the Club Baby Grand, and the Spot Grille on French Street.

Somewhere in the mix, he'd hung out in New York City and did a stint with the Boyd Raeburn Band, but in Wilmington, he fell into his element. Among the earliest local musicians he ran into was Lem Winchester. The year was 1946, and Bob met Lem on the third floor of the building that included the Spot, which was just below street level. Lem had just become interested in playing the vibes, and for some reason, there was a set of them upstairs, as well as a set of them inside the club itself. Lem was a quick study, and while whistling the tunes he heard in his head, he became proficient, soon excelling on the instrument.

Lem Winchester was part of the larger Davis and Wilkerson families, both of which had intermarried members, and many of them were involved in the local jazz scene throughout the early 1950s.

Lem's sister Millie Wilkerson, later known as Millie Cannon, began her career as a jazz singer in 1951 with jazz pianist Preston Johnson's Mood Mixers, then with jazz saxophonist Charley Robinson's Jazz Men. Millie even had the opportunity to audition with the Lionel Hampton Band but turned the offer down for various reasons. Millie had a long relationship with Preston into the 1970s, eventually marrying him.

Others who were members of the greater Davis and Wilkerson families were Joe Davis and George Wilkerson. Joe Davis, a jazz bassist, had his own trio that included guitarist Doug Holland and pianist Gerald Price, and he backed Millie Cannon on several occasions. George Wilkerson, Lem and Millie's brother, became a noted drummer; he passed in 2016.

Gerald "Junie" Price, a jazz pianist, also made an impression during the late 1940s and throughout the 1950s. He played with Clifford Brown, Bob Cordrey, and later with local jazz musicians Len Foster, Deanie Jenkins, and Bop Wilson at many venues.

There were several notable jazz clubs in post-World War II Wilmington. The Club Baby Grand had changed its name from the Club Harlem. The Spot Grille had closed in 1954, and others had not survived the War. One new club that became popular in 1953 when it opened was the Sans Souci at 14th & King Streets. Operated by Marian Allen, the Sans Souci was openly integrated during those times when the unspoken Jim Crow policies were enforced by Wilmington's hospitality businesses. Lem Winchester played at the Sans Souci often, keeping his vibes there so that while walking the beat as a cop nearby he could call in for a break and duck into the Sans Souci to work out the tune he had been whistling while pounding the streets.

Tragedy had struck the Winchester household on December 3rd, 1952, when Lem and his wife Beulah lost their eight-month-old son, Lemuel Jr., to "acute pulmonary congestion," what today we might call "sudden infant death syndrome." Things were quiet from Lem Winchester musically until that day when Clifford Brown died.

In September of 1956, Lem played a major role, along with local music legend Claude Wells, in a Clifford Brown Memorial Scholarship Fund concert. Announced in the national jazz periodical *Downbeat,* the concert was held at the Brandywine Music Box just across the Pennsylvania state line at Route 1 and 202. Scheduled to play were Max Roach, Sahib Shihab, Sonny Stitt, Jimmy Smith, Lou Donaldson, Sarah Vaughan, and Dinah Washington.

In 1957, Lem Winchester took part in a Jazz Workshop Concert at the Wilmington Drama League Theatre on Lea Boulevard. Music included the local Dick Kenny Quartet with Gerald Price on piano.

From June 8th through June 14th, 1957, the earliest incarnation of the Lem Winchester's Modernists performed at the Parkway Lounge on Route 13 just south of Wilmington. Later in June, Lem and Gerald Price, who were the core musicians of the Modernists, performed at the Arden Guild Hall with many other notable musicians in what was billed as "Cabaret Night with Don Elliott Versatile Jazz Artist of TV Recording Fame and His Quartet." Elliott specialized on the mellophone and had cut albums nationally on the RCA and ABC Paramount labels. It would not be the only time he would perform in the Wilmington area.

Later that summer, Lem got to play with a trio of college kids, two of whom, Dave Arnold on bass and John Chowning on drums, were from Wilmington. The two, along with pianist George Lindamood, were students at Wittenberg College in Springfield, Ohio. During the late summer of 1957, the trio called The Collegiates, performed at Marshall's Restaurant in Wilmington's Merchandize Mart on the Governor Printz Boulevard. The main attraction playing with John Chowning's Collegiates was Lem Winchester, with Gerald Price occasionally sitting in. The gig ended on August 27th as a farewell to the Collegiates who had to return to school in Ohio. However, the next day, August 28th, the Trio joined Lem Winchester for a recording session at RCA's main recording studios in New York City. It would be Lem's first commercial recording session, and though unsuccessful as an RCA release, it got Lem Winchester noticed.

Despite apparently being on the verge of success, Lem Winchester was still a Wilmington Police Officer. On October 4th, 1957, the same day that the Soviet Union launched Sputnik into earth orbit at the dawning of the Space Age, Lem made an arrest. In fact, it's the only arrest for which we have a record because it was reported in *The Wilmington Morning News*. The hapless victim was Herman Henry, who was living nearby in the Walnut Street YMCA.

Henry was in the Club Baby Grand selling joints out of his hatband. Lem, who was off duty and in his street clothes, was enjoying himself in the Baby Grand when Herman Henry made the mistake of approaching him with an offer. To make the sale, the two went into the restroom, a facility that Mitch Thomas once told me was one of the rankest places he had ever been. It was there that Henry attempted to sell him four joints before Lem collared him. At the police station, six more joints were found hidden in Henry's hat.

The next day, October 5th, Lem and his Modernists shared a venue with mellophonist Don Elliott, another multi-instrumentalist, at the Shriner's Auditorium on Route 13 near the New Castle County Airport for what was billed as the "Delaware Jazz Workshop's Cabaret

Night." It's not hard to imagine that Lem and Don Elliott, who also played vibes, may have compared some notes.

The first big event for Lem Winchester occurred nine months later at the Newport Jazz Festival in Rhode Island, July 6th, 1958. The festival had opened the previous day with the Duke Ellington Orchestra, featuring Mahalia Jackson. Others participating were the Benny Goodman Band, Dave Brubeck, Cannonball Adderley, Gerry Mulligan, Mary Lou Williams, Maynard Ferguson, Pete Johnson, Big Maybelle with Jack Teagarden, Chuck Berry, and R&B pioneer Julia Lee.

Since he had not brought his coterie of local musicians, Lem was accompanied at the event by Ray Santisi on piano, John Neves on bass, and Jimmy Zitano on drums. He was introduced by jazz composer, musician, and impresario Leonard Feather. The quartet played only three tunes: Charlie Parker's "Now's the Time," a standard and favorite of Lem's, "Polkadots and Moonbeams," and the Billy Strayhorn tune "Take the 'A' Train." The audience and the critics alike were wowed.

Two other events occurred later in 1958, within a week of one another, both significant to the local jazz scene. The first was Lem Winchester's first full album, on the Argo label. He had shared his first commercial recording, *New Faces at Newport 1958,* with Randy Weston on the flip side. This time Lem was heard on both sides, along with three astute jazz musicians from Chicago known as the Ramsey Lewis Trio. With Lewis on piano, El Dee Young on bass, Red Holt on drums, and Lem on vibes. This October 8th recording was tagged as *A Tribute to Clifford Brown.* It included Brownie's "Sandu," his "Joy Spring," Lem's first recorded composition "Where It Is," and a composition by Boysie Lowery, "A Message from Boysie."

One week later, on October 15th, that other event would rattle the local jazz scene. It was the day that Thelonious Monk came to town, but not to play.

Riding through Wilmington to a gig in Baltimore was Baroness Kathleen DeKoenigswarter in her Bentley. With her in the car were Thelonious Monk and saxophonist Charlie Rouse. Monk wasn't feeling well, so he asked to stop and get some water. They had the misfortune to stop at a motel in Minquadale. To make a long story short, they were accosted by the local police, who found a small amount of marijuana on Monk and in the Baroness' luggage. Monk was beaten by the police for refusing to get out of the car, during which time DeKoenigswarter warned the cops not to break Monk's hands because he made his living playing the piano. The three were arraigned in Magistrate Court. After a bond of $5,000 was paid, a court date was set for April 1960. At that later date, Monk was fined $110.00 for assaulting a police officer.

In that recorded interview with Scott Davidson, Marian Allen said that jazz notables Sarah Vaughan, Dinah Washington, and Thelonious Monk had visited the Sans Souci, not to perform but only to dig the music and ambiance. Could either that 1958 incident or the 1960 court date that followed had been when Monk dropped in? One has to wonder.

Illustrations

Willard Burns Chippey, shown here playing the violbone, an instrument of his own invention, was a musician in Paul F. Thompson's Dixieland Band from the early 20th century in Wilmington. Thompson's band had the distinction to be an integrated ensemble.
Courtesy of Delaware Historical Society

The Radio Boys, later to become Henry "Peck" Morris' Radio Boys. The band was Wilmington's first fully developed jazz band in the 1920s. Henry "Peck" Morris is the second from the left, with the trumpet.
Courtesy of Morris family Archive

Sam Wooding's Chocolate Dandies. Wooding is in the center sitting in the easy chair. (public domain)

Betty Roché, born in Wilmington on January 9, 1920, was the first local artist to record nationally, first with the Savoy Sultans but mostly with Duke Ellington in the 1940s to early 50s. She had three solo albums in the mid 1950s and early 1960s. (public domain)

The Spot at 703 French Street, interior and exterior

'A Merry Christmas To All
CLUB HARLEM
9th & Poplar Sts.
featuring
Jimmy Hinsley & His Maniacs Of Rhythm
BERNICE BURNS — DAISY WINCHESTER

SEASON'S GREETINGS
COLEMAN ALLEN
Tenor Sax
ARTIE WELLS' BAND

Ads from the Wilmington Herald Times December 1941 University of Delaware Morris Library microfilm

Greetings From
JOE THOMAS
And His
ROYAL SWINGSTERS
Now Appearing At The
SPOT GRILLE
703 FRENCH STREET
Wilmington, Del.

The Deuces of Rhythm. On baton, likely Laddie Springs. Front row L-R: Louis Randolph, Robert "Boysie" Lowery, Mr. Horse Collar, Billy Jackson, & Bud Lowery. Back row L-R: Jimmy Turner, Robert Townsend, & Daisy Winchester, who in 1940 recorded "You've Got to go When the Wagon Comes" with emerging recording artist Louis Jordan and his Tympany Five. Photo likely at Club Harlem, (Club Baby Grand after World War II). Courtesy of Scott Davidson Archive

Robert "Boysie" Lowery, musician, teacher, and mentor to nearly every Wilmington jazz musician from Clifford Brown and Lem Winchester to those who continue to play jazz to this day.
(public domain)

Rob Cordrey, Ralph Morris, and Preston Johnson played together in the 1940s
Photo credits—lt: obituary; ctr: Steven Leech; rt: Floyd VonRiper

Ralph Morris, left, with Clifford Brown
Courtesy of Scott Davidson Archive

Photos of Clifford Brown/Max Roach Quintet at Baby Grand
Courtesy of Scott Davidson Archive

Maurice Sims was Wilmington's second Black radio DJ at WTUX and the first to broadcast Clifford Brown's first recording of "Ida Red."
Gloria Rashada,
Delaware Valley Star

In a photo taken in the Club Baby Grand, on the right is Ida Mae Wade, Clifford Brown's lady friend who inspired his first commercial recording, "Ida Red," with Chris Powell and the Blue Flames in 1952. In the center is Irvin Sims, Maurice Sims' older brother, with his wife Virginia.
Courtesy of Scott Davidson archive

Lem Winchester
Scott Davidson archive

Mitch Thomas, Delaware's first Black radio personality, often acted as Master of Ceremonies at the Club Baby Grand. He also had a Saturday afternoon dance show on local television.
Courtesy of Michael Thomas

Lem Winchester with his adoptive parents, William J. and Bessie Winchester
Courtesy of Scott Davidson archive

The Joe Davis Trio. Joe is playing bass on the left. Preston Johnson on piano and vibes in the center, and Doug Holland on guitar. It was on Preston Johnson's vibraphone that Lem Winchester began to learn to play the instrument. Photo was probably taken in The Spot, 703 French Street in Wilmington.
Courtesy of Scott Davidson archive

Lem Winchester, Wilmington police officer by day, jazz musician by night, though often he whistled a tune on his beat, sometimes ducking into the Sans Souci to work out a tune on the vibes he kept stored there.
Courtesy of Maurice Sims Archive

Lem Winchester, on the left, with an early ensemble consisting of Doug Holland on guitar, Danny Settles on bass, Preston Johnson on piano, and Coleman Allen on saxophone.
Courtesy of Scott Davidson Archive

Millie Cannon with the Al Cato Trio at the Roundtable Inn near 12th & King Streets in Wilmington.
Courtesy of Scott Davidson Archive

Millie Cannon with the Al Cato Trio. On the left is Jim Salvatori on drums, Al Cato on bass, Millie Cannon, and Ken Steir on piano.
Courtesy of Scott Davidson Archive

Jazz singer Millie Cannon with the Al Cato Quintette. Behind Millie, from the left are Deanie Jenkins on piano, Ron Smith on tenor saxophone, Purcell Street on alto saxophone, Stan Williams on drums, and Al Cato on bass. Ron Smith's father, Chick Smith, had his own band in the late 1930s and early 40s. He'd been in high demand from other local bands during this time period as an arranger.
Courtesy of Scott Davidson Archive

Marian Allen owned the Sans Souci at 14th & King Streets in Wilmington. Her club, kind of like the Café Society in New York City, welcomed jazz lovers from all backgrounds, and kept the local jazz vibe going into the early 1970s.
Courtesy of the Linda Sobieski Archive

At the *Sans Souci*

Two candid photos from the *Sans Souci*

On the left, Preston Johnson at the piano accompanying singer Rose Montgomery.
Courtesy of the Linda Sobieski Archive

On the right, Lem Winchester on vibraphone.
Courtesy of Delaware Historical Society

William (Dutch) Burton, shown seated here with Ralph Morris at the piano, was a Wilmington City Councilman who was refused service in 1958 in a Wilmington restaurant under the city's Jim Crow policies, while clubs like the Club Baby Grand and the Sans Souci welcomed patronage without discrimination. After Burton sued, the U. S. Supreme Court finally ruled in his favor in 1961.

photo by Steven Leech

After Ralph Morris was refused service as a guest on radio pioneer Joe Pyne's radio show, which he broadcasted live in a local restaurant, Pyne threatened to immediately end his broadcast if Ralph was not served. The restaurant relented and Ralph was served.
(public domain)

The Modernists with Danny Settles on bass, Gerald Price on piano, Lem Winchester on vibes, Billy Davis on drums, and Sylvester (Papa Dee) Allen on congas.
Both photos courtesy of Scott Davidson archive.
Below the Modernists perform at Saint Andrew's School in March 1960.

Wilmington jazz pianist Gerald "Junie" Price, shown on the right and below with jazz singer Justine Keeys, known professionally as Miss Justine, with whom he recorded and performed. After moving to Philadelphia to keep his career alive, Gerald recorded with Richie Cole and Sonny Stitt as well as performing with and mentoring many up and coming jazz artists. He performed at Wilmington's The Flight Deck on the day the venue close down for good.

All photos courtesy of the Morris family archive

MISS JUSTINE

A New Generation of Wilmington Jazz Artists

The Boysie Lowery Alumni Band
From the left: Gerald Chavis, Vernon James, Leander Howell, Larry Williams, Joe Kearney, Harry Spencer, Nate Davenport, Gregory Robinson, Darryl Payton, Gregory Davis, James Dixon, and Joe "Sly" Smithers.
Courtesy of Larry Williams Archive

Wilby Fletcher

Larry Unthank

Fletcher Memorial Brochure

(Public Domain)

Chapter Five

Jes Grew, Jim Crow, and the Wrecking Ball

Jes Grew infects all that it touches.
—Ishmael Reed, *Mumbo Jumbo*

Late in 1958, Lem Winchester's LP with the Ramsey Lewis Trio was released. By then, he had formed the band with whom he would perform except for several appearances with the Manny Klein Trio at the Holiday Inn at 1843 Marsh Road in October and November. Manny Klein, who played piano, later served as President of the Musicians' Union from 1975 to 1983.

Lem's first band, The Modernists, were then Gerald Price on piano, Billy Davis on drums, Danny Settles on bass, and Sylvester "Papa Dee" Allen on percussion. Probably the first appearance of this lineup was at the New Castle County Air Base Enlisted Men's Club on November 1st, 1958. On May 21st, 1959, the Modernist performed at the Dunleith School auditorium.

Beginning August 24th, 1959, Lem and the Modernists began to perform nightly at the Club Baby Grand. Within a month, Lem had signed on with Prestige Records and began making the trip to their recording studio at Englewood Cliffs, New Jersey, to record commercially with some of the top-shelf artists in jazz.

Lem's first album *Winchester Special* was recorded on September 25th, 1959, with tenor saxophonist Benny Golson, Tommy Flanagan on piano, Wendell Marshall on bass, and Arthur Taylor on drums. The LP included two tunes written by Winchester: "The Dude" and "Down Fuzz," which in today's parlance can be translated into "cool cop," and which yielded a 45 rpm on the New Jazz label. The album also included the tune "Mysticism," composed by Wilmington musician Len Foster.

By the time 1960 rolled around, Wilmington was once again a full-swing, cookin' town. New venues where jazz was heard were popping up in the city. Besides the Club Baby Grand and the Sans Souci, which had opened its door in 1953 at 14th and King Street, another club was the Bali

Hai on New Castle Avenue and Rogers Road, where the city runs into the largely Black suburban development of Dunleith. Another club was the Roundtable at 12th and King Streets.

Maurice Sims said he remembers Lem Winchester performing at the Roundtable with local pianist Deanie Jenkins and alto saxophonist Purcell Street. Purcell even did a little singing, Maurice reported. It was the final time Maurice saw Lem perform.

A few other places that featured jazz on the Eastside were Kilroy's Tavern at 329 East 4th Street and the Midtown Grill at 4 East 4th Street. That wasn't the end of it. There'd been a number of informal after-hours second- and third-floor jazz spots throughout the city.

One thing in common with all jazz venues is that they welcomed jazz fans no matter the color of one's skin, especially the Sans Souci —Wilmington's answer to the Café Society in New York City. Not so much with Wilmington's Eagle Restaurant at 9th and Shipley Streets.

The decade of the 1960s was primed by a controversy regarding Wilmington City Councilman William F. "Dutch" Burton when he was refused service at the Eagle Restaurant in 1958. The event spawned a lawsuit litigated by attorney Louis Redding, one of the litigants in the 1954 Brown v. Board of Education decision by the U. S. Supreme Court. On January 11th, 1960, the Delaware Supreme Court ruled that the Eagle Restaurant could discriminate, overruling a prior Chancellery Court ruling. The case eventually ended up in the U. S. Supreme Court, which in 1961 overruled the decision by the Delaware Supreme Court and led to legislation passed by the Kennedy Administration regarding public accommodations. This wasn't the only public display of lingering and largely unspoken Jim Crow policies in Wilmington.

Ralph Morris, the youngest brother of 1930s bandleader Henry "Peck" Morris and a member of Bob Cordrey's jazz combo, told me a story of how he'd been a guest on the Joe Pyne radio show, broadcasting from a Wilmington Restaurant around the same time as the Burton incident. Joe Pyne was a pioneer of "talk radio" and did a live show on WILM.

During the broadcast, Pyne offered Ralph a drink, but the restaurant refused Ralph service. The way Ralph told the story, Pyne declared that he'd pull the plug and abruptly end the broadcast if Ralph were not served. Ralph got his drink.

So, while Jim Crow was slowly dying on Wilmington's west side, Jes Grew had been bringing social and cultural progress on the Eastside, which was on the eve of destruction.

Lem Winchester continued to walk the beat, whistling a tune, greeting those he knew with a wave and a broad smile, occasionally stopping at a call box to take a break and duck into the Sans Souci where he stored his vibes and work out some improvisation on a tune that was banging around in his head.

As far back as the early 1950s, local "urban developers" and politicians were making plans and scheming to "renew" the urban landscape of the east side of Wilmington. Eventually, the plan was to demolish 22 blocks, pointing out that *some* structures were in decay, without plumbing, and still had outhouses. However, many houses had been up to code and contained families, and the many businesses there supported the local economy. But the die had been cast, so before the year was over, the bulldozers and the wrecking ball moved in and began to seal the fate of the Eastside. Among the sites to be demolished was the historic AUMP Church at 8th and French Streets, founded by Peter Spencer in 1813 and the source of the oldest African American celebration in the United States, the August Quarterly. Also set for demolition were the National Theater—later the Hopkins—and many of those jazz clubs like the Spot Grille. Some of those streets where Lem was used to walking his beat would soon disappear.

Despite the encroaching maul of "Negro removal," as many residents would call "urban renewal," the beat went on.

On February 15th, 1960, Lem and the Modernists performed at the Club Baby Grand. On March 3rd, the Modernists piled into the hearse Lem had bought, otherwise known as a Cadillac station wagon, with room enough for five of them plus Lem's vibes, a string bass, conga drums, and a drum kit, and headed for an out-of-town gig at the Red Hill Inn in Pennsauken, New Jersey. They would be substituting for Max Roach, who had problems getting out of Pittsburgh. Also in March, the Modernist played a concert at St. Andrew's School in Middletown, Delaware. On March 17th Lem and the Modernists began performing regularly at the Sans Souci. On March 22nd, Lem once again headed for Englewood Cliffs, New Jersey, to record with tenor saxophonist Oliver Nelson, Johnny "Hammond" Smith on organ, George Tucker on bass, and Roy Haynes on drums for Nelson's LP *Takin' Care of Business*. Less than a month later, on April 19th, Lem would return to Prestige's studio to record his next solo album, *Lem's Beat*, with Oliver Nelson, Curtis Peagler on alto, Bill Brown and Roy Johnson on piano, Wendell Marshall on bass, and Arthur Taylor on drums.

While the wind had begun to whirl around

Lem Winchester's musical career, things were hopping at the Club Baby Grand. On April 29th, Thornell Schwartz, who had accompanied Jimmy Smith on that August 4th, 1956, gig at the Baby Grand, made an appearance. On May 20th Crazy Chris Colombo did a gig at the Club Baby Grand, and on June 5th, vibraphonist Johnny Lytle appeared there with his trio.

The day before, on June 4th, Lem again ventured to the Prestige studios to record his *Another Opus* LP with Frank Wess on flute and tenor sax, Hank Jones on piano, Eddie Jones on bass, and Gus Johnson on drums. The album included three of Lem's own compositions: "Another Opus," "Both Barrels," and "Blues Prayer."

Also during the summer of 1960, Lem performed at the Birmingham Jazz Festival, just outside of Detroit, Michigan. He performed three tunes, Milt Jackson's "Bluesology" and the standards "Like Someone In Love" and "Softly, as in a Morning Sunrise." His accompanying musicians were Junior Mance on piano, J.C. Heard on drums, and Nick Fiore on bass. The recording, preserved on a Consolidated Artists Production CD (CAP 291), includes the only known recording of Lem Winchester speaking.

On June 21st, Lem was back at the Prestige studios to record with jazz organist Shirley Scott on the *Soul Sister* album. With Lem and Shirley were bassist George Duvivier and Arthur Edgehill on drums. On July 12th, he recorded an LP with organist Jack McDuff that included Jimmy Forrest on tenor sax and Bill Elliott on drums. On August 23rd, he recorded with saxophonist Oliver Nelson on his *Nocturne* album, with Richard Wyands on piano, George Duvivier on bass, and Roy Haynes on drums. On September 16th, Lem recorded with the same musicians, backing singer Etta Jones for her *Something Nice* LP. A single from that album, "Canadian Sunset," was a national hit for one week on the Billboard chart in March 1961.

Still in the summer of 1960 and into the autumn season, things were still cookin' at the Club Baby Grand. In a July 4th matinee, veteran jazz singer and organist Sarah McLawler and jazz violinist Richard Otto performed their unique style of music. Jazz and R&B guitarist Tiny Grimes, who had recorded with Billie Holiday and the Cats and the Fiddle, among many others, appeared there on July 15th. Jimmy McGriff came to play on July 22nd. In a slightly different style of music, singers Don Gardner and Dee Dee Ford appeared at the Baby Grand on August 26th, and vibraphonist Johnny Lytle had a return performance on September 26th.

The Jodimars, former members of the Comets—who had walked out on Bill Haley in

1955 to sign with another record label—were performers at the Bali Hai on September 2nd. Millie Cannon, who had been performing in Clubs from Philadelphia to Baltimore, starred in a "Gala Evening" on September 2nd at the Wilmington Armory at 10th and DuPont Streets, sponsored by the NAACP.

By the summer of 1960, Lem's performing and recording schedule was beginning to jeopardize his day job as a Wilmington police officer. Any number of jazz critics and reviewers were suggesting publicly that he would have to decide which career he wanted to keep. By the same token, trying to mesh his police and music careers profoundly affected his home life with Beulah and their sons. Push had to come to shove, and Lem submitted his resignation on July 18th, 1960, becoming official on July 22nd.

Lem Winchester recorded what would be his final solo album *With Feeling* on October 7th, 1960, sometimes referred to as the "Moodsville" album. Lem was accompanied by Richard Wyands on piano, George Duvivier on bass, and Roy Haynes on drums. Lem also wrote "The Kids" for the album.

Lem would, however, perform as a sideman for one final album by organist Johnny "Hammond" Smith. Recorded on October 14th, 1960, *Talk That Talk* also included Eddie McFadden on guitar, Wendell Marshall on bass, and Bill Erskine on drums.

The month of December 1960 began with Lem and the Modernists piling into his converted hearse for a gig in Pittsburgh at the Hurricane Bar at 1603 Centre Avenue. They were there performing on the 3rd and 4th of that month.

Later in December, no one would ever suspect that Lem Winchester and the Modernists would be performing their final engagement at the Club Baby Grand.

Unlike his predecessor Clifford Brown, Lem Winchester did not tour with professional musicians from disparate parts of the jazz world. He only recorded with them. He performed live, whether locally or elsewhere, with a band totally made up of local musicians, each one having honed their chops from a long history of playing together in Wilmington. Two of them, Gerald Price and Papa Dee Allen, would go on to record commercially with nationally known musical artists. In a sense, unlike Clifford Brown, Lem Winchester might have continued a recording career with all Wilmington musicians, something rare in recorded jazz at the time. Unfortunately, we'll never know what the Modernists sounded like. There are no known recordings of the Modernists, adding to the list of music missing from the archives, like all local music performed by Wilmington jazz musicians before 1940 and like the single performance of Clifford Brown and Charlie Parker playing together. It has all evaporated into the ether.

A few days before January 13th, 1961, the Modernists piled into Lem's hearse with all their instruments and headed for their gig in Indianapolis, Indiana, their farthest engagement from home. Great expectations accompanied them, including the possibility that the band might one day record commercially.

On the first night of their performance at the Topper Club and Lounge in Indianapolis, Lem made one fatal mistake after the first set. One story is that Gerald Price had a toothache, and Lem went to find some aspirin. One of those from whom he inquired was the club's bartender Robert Cook. Noticing that Cook kept a pistol in a drawer in the cash register, temptation played its hand. It was Friday the 13th in a year that read the same upside down. That should've been a sign.

The bartender's revolver was a Smith & Wesson .38 snubnose. Lem told Cook he'd show him a trick he'd used to scare people, daredevil that Lem was, and he prepared the pistol with only one round among the remaining empty chambers. Lem spun the cylinder counting the clicks in the cylinder's ratchet, then put the revolver under his chin and squeezed the trigger.

The sound was like a loud slam of a huge door. The single round went through the top of Lem's head and pinged around the room a couple of times. Lem tried to run in disbelief, but one foot was anchored to the floor. He made two or three steps in a circle then collapsed on the floor, bleeding out.

Can't undo this one this time. If only he had known that the cylinder on a Smith & Wesson had revolved in the opposite direction from the Colt .38 police revolver he had used to perform the trick before. In the twenty final minutes before the ambulance arrived, Lem tried to remember himself. By then, it was too late.

Four days later, reportedly, thousands of mourners attempted to crowd into the Mount Joy Methodist Church at B and Townsend Streets, just as they had at Bell's Funeral Home the night before. Later that day Lem Winchester was interred at the Mount Zion Cemetery where Clifford Brown had been been laid to rest four and a half years before.

The jazz world was stunned. Another up-and-coming jazz genius from Wilmington was cut down after barely a three-year career. Clifford Brown had been only 25 years old when he died. Lem Winchester was only 32 years old.

On January 24th, 1961, Wilmington native

Betty Roché recorded her final album *Lightly and Politely*. In an act of coincidental serendipity, one of the songs on this final album was her rendition of the standard "Polka Dots and Moonbeams." It was one of Lem's favorite tunes and one he chose to perform on his first commercial recording from the 1958 Newport Jazz Festival two and a half years before. Adding to this, Papa Dee Allen performed with the Manny Klein Trio at the Holiday Inn while also performing solo at The Attic, one of the city's coffee house venues that were popping up due to the emerging folk music revival in the early 1960s. Papa Dee would later move to California and realize success with the rock band WAR, fronted by former Animals singer Eric Burdon. On February 11th, 1961, the Modernists performed at the Holiday Inn, and the following week, February 18th, they performed at the Club Baby Grand with Jerry Berkowitz on vibes. On August 17th, 1961, remnants of the Modernists with Preston Johnson on piano and with Kelly Williams, a singer who had been a mainstay at the Sans Souci, performed at the Crescendo in Camden, New Jersey. By then, the wrecking ball and the bulldozers were chewing up the Eastside, turning block after block into rubble.

Chapter Six
The Day Junie Left Town

We're not referring to a specific date, though Gerald "Junie" Price did leave town on a day in 1966, the same year the Club Baby Grand closed its doors. There were many momentous days in the 1960s. The day when 22 blocks finally lay barren on the Eastside. The day the Club Baby Grand finally closed its doors. The day Clifford Brown's family home at 1013 Poplar Street was torn down, leaving it to this day the only vacant lot on the block. The day Boysie Lowery had to move from his home on Pine Street to Broom Street on the city's west side.

Junie left town because there hadn't been enough places left in the city where he could play. The Eastside was gone. One of the only opportunities to perform was with emerging rock and roll performer Lue Cazz (Lou Casapulla) on some unreleased recordings. Lue Cazz had cut some 45 rpms on various labels, and once performed at St. Anthony's auditorium with Boysie Lowery and up-and-coming musician and producer Jerome Jefferson.

In fact, the beat went on after the destruction of the Eastside and the tragic death of Lem Winchester had put a dent in the local jazz scene. Rhythm & blues and rock & roll became the new beat in the early 1960s when it became economically feasible to produce single 45 rpm records in Wilmington and not depend on out-of-town record producers of 33 & 1/3 LPs. People like Vinnie Rago would produce local R&B artists like Teddy & the Continentals, The Continettes, Lonnie & the Crisis, Johnny & the Dreams, and others without even having a place of business. Local music producer James J. Chavis produced local groups like the Spidels and the Grand Prees on his Candi and Chavis labels. Several smaller local record producers were putting out 45 RPMs. But all that entrepreneurial musical effort came to a screeching halt after the assassination of Martin Luther King, the riots that followed, and the nine months of martial law in Wilmington in the aftermath.

Another talented jazz musician to leave

town in the 1960s was alto saxophonist Harry Spencer. Spencer ventured a bit farther than Junie Price, heading all the way to New York City. Harry eventually joined up with Sun Ra before making it back to Wilmington. He can be heard on Sun Ra's *Magic City* LP delivering a scorching solo on the title selection.

Venues on the west side of Wilmington still didn't have a welcoming feel for local Black jazz musicians. Beside the Bali Hai, which became the Dutch Tavern in the mid-1960s on Wilmington's southeast fringe, the only clubs downtown where jazz musicians from diverse backgrounds could play were the Club Baby Grand, which hung on through the early 60s despite the destruction wrought by the Poplar Street A Project that ended right across 9th Street, the Sans Souci, five blocks north at 14th and King, and the Roundtable at 12th and King Streets.

It was at the Roundtable that Lem Winchester's sister Millie Cannon and a trio formed by bassist Al Cato performed regularly while playing gigs at other venues in adjoining states. Al Cato used an array of local musicians to form his combos, whether as a trio, quartet, or quintet, including Ron Smith on tenor, Purcell Street on alto, Deanie Jenkins or Ken Steir on piano, Jim Salvatori or Stan Williams on drums—all veteran jazz musician during the 1950s. The

Sans Souci kept going by providing a looser venue, and by that we mean accommodating musicians, whether regular or up-and-coming ones, with regular jam sessions, particularly on Saturday afternoons. The Sans Souci hung on throughout the 1960s but suffered the same fate as did the city's locally produced R&B and rock & roll when the riots and martial law transpired in 1968 as well as the protracted public transportation strike of 1967. The Sans Souci hobbled along but finally had to close its doors in 1973.

Junie Price's move to Philadelphia in 1966 proved to be successful for him. Not only did he have the opportunity to mentor a number of emerging musicians like the group Pieces of a Dream, but he performed with the likes of Dakota Staton, Sarah Vaughan, Sammy Davis, Jr., Joe Williams, and Zoot Sims.

While in Philadelphia, Price formed a trio consisting of himself, Benny Nelson on bass, and Al Jackson on drums. In 1975 his trio recorded an album with Richie Cole on saxophone, Cole's impossible-to-find first album *Trenton Makes, The World Takes*. In 1979, Junie ventured to Paris, France, to record an album with the venerable jazz saxophonist Sonny Stitt on his *The Definitive Black & Blue Sessions,* recorded on November 12th. Don Mosley on bass and Bobby Durham on drums rounded out the quartet. Around the same time, that same ensemble, with the addition of Milt Jackson on vibes, recorded a live session for one of Stitt's *Loose Walk* series. It may have been the only example of what Junie and Lem might have sounded like together. Like Lem Winchester and Clifford Brown, Junie wrote some tunes. He reportedly wrote a theme song for the Modernists. While most of Junie's compositions fall into the category of "missing music," one of his songs was recorded by Grover Washington Jr. on his 1982 album *The Best Is Yet to Come* on the Electra label. The tune was "Things Are Getting Better," and Junie's lyrics were sung by Bobby McFerrin.

Meanwhile in Wilmington, the city's jazz legacy was kept alive with a commemorative concert staged in the newly renovated Grand Opera House on June 26th, 1976, produced by historian Harmon Carey twenty years to the day after the death of Clifford Brown. Clifford's first bandmate, pianist Donald Criss, having changed his name to Rashid Yaya, led the ensemble that performed at the event. Noted trumpet player and former Boysie Lowery student Marcus Belgrave played, as well as local musicians Vernon James and Charles Bowen on saxophones, Joe Kearney on bass, Richard Holmes on drums, James Dixon on trumpet, Atiba on percussion, and vocalist Rashida Yaya.

A limited-edition LP was produced as a result of the event and included several selections from it. Partly because some technical kinks prevailed due to the very recent opening of the renovated Grand Opera House, the recording was less than perfect. One of the performances left out of the finished LP featured Boysie Lowery, who had taught and mentored nearly every jazz musician in Wilmington, and even a few rock & roll musicians like Lue Cazz. Because the recording was flawed, Boysie donated a recording of a practice session from the late 1940s made in his basement where he taught his students, one of whom was Clifford Brown. The cut with only Boysie and Clifford playing was Charlie Parker's "Ornithology." In recent years, the recording has sprouted legs and may be found on any number of compact discs that contain rare or live recordings by Clifford Brown. It may be the only extant recording of Boysie Lowery.

In the early 1980s, Junie began mentoring a jazz singer in Philadelphia named Justine Keeys, who performed and recorded under the name of Miss Justine. The two of them performed together often in the Philadelphia area. One of their live recordings, "You Do," can be found on Miss Justine's *Tasty* CD from 1998.

In 1983 Junie Price returned briefly to perform at The Flight Deck, a popular jazz club opened initially at the New Castle County Airport on Route 13 near Hare's Corner. When Junie appeared there in 1983, The Flight Deck had moved into center city Wilmington at 5th and Market Streets. It would be the final show before The Flight Deck closed. Despite attempts to revive the city, years of urban abuse by the powers-that-be would make those attempts impossible.

    Gerald "Junie" Price died in February 1996 from pancreatic cancer. It was a bad year because in September Robert "Boysie" Lowery followed Junie to that big gig in the Great Beyond.

Chapter Seven

From Boysie's Basement to the Flight Deck

Two threads wind their way through this story of Wilmington jazz. The first is the amount of music that is missing amongst all that was made in Wilmington before 1940, from the Brown/Parker performance to music produced by Lem Winchester's Modernists and, tragically, the music of Clifford Brown in collaboration with Lem Winchester and others like Gerald Price. If only Brownie and Lem had lived to continue their careers. Imagine a jazz ensemble recording featuring Clifford Brown, Lem Winchester, Junie Price, and others with Betty Roché and Millie Cannon sharing singing duties. The prospect is staggering and could have put Wilmington on the country's jazz map.

One name that constantly comes up is Queen Belle, along with her accompanist on tenor sax, Wilson Smith. From what's been told about her, she was evidently a very accomplished and popular jazz artist. However, no recordings of her performance have yet to be found. More missing music.

The second thread is the enormous role that Boysie Lowery has had in the story of Wilmington jazz. From the early 1940s to his passing in 1996, he mentored, taught, and influenced nearly every jazz musician to have earned his or her chops in Wilmington.

Beginning with the most recent success story among Boysie's students is tenor saxophonist Fostina Dixon, who has enjoyed two of her recent recordings entering the national Billboard music charts at the time of this report. The most enduring former student of Boysie Lowery is saxaphoonist Ernie Watts. Though a student of Boysie's in his early years growing up in Wilmington, Ernie went on to study music at West Chester University and Berklee College of Music, which led to a very successful career. Not only has he toured with the Rolling Stones and recorded with Frank Zappa, Marvin Gaye, and Sarah Vaughan, but he was part of Doc Severinsen's Tonight Show band. His performances have been heard in many television and movie soundtracks as well.

Another Boysie Lowery student is Matthew Shipp, a successful jazz pianist forging new ground in avant-garde jazz as well as hip-hop culture, as demonstrated by his collaboration with DJ Spooky.

Had he lived beyond his sudden, unexpected death, Wilby Fletcher most certainly would have gained greater success. Wilby was another Boysie Lowery student, as was his father, saxophonist Wilby Fletcher, Sr. The young Wilby recorded with jazz bassist Ron Carter, among others, and performed with jazz pianists McCoy Tyner and Michel Petrucciani, as well as locally with a number of Boysie Lowery's Delaware students. Wilby recorded with multi-instrumentalist Dexter Koonce, Boysie's nephew, and Koonce's singing partner Alfie Moss, also a Boysie Lowery student.

Boysie's influence and mentorship extended to any number of local musicians already mentioned, like Harry Spenser, Vernon James, who collaborated with Gil-Scott Heron on his *Reflections* album, and multi-instrumentalist Len Foster, who composed "Mysticism" on Lem Winchester's *Winchester Special* LP. For a short time, Lue Cazz (Casapulla) was a student, as was Joe Harris, tenor saxophonist who played a large part in Wilmington's R&B and rock & roll presence in the 1960s.

Before we continue, we ought to mention who Boysie considered his best student, tenor saxophonist Charles Robinson. Coleman Allen, a contemporary of Robinson, was also a student of Boysie. Allen played in one of Wilmington's earliest jazz bands, the Claude and Artie Wells Band, but he continued to sharpen his chops under Boysie's tutelage.

Clifford Brown's earliest bandmate Donald Criss (a.k.a. Rashid Yaya) was a Boysie Lowery student, as were Lem Winchester's accompanists Gerald Price, Deanie Jenkins, Billy Davis, and Papa Dee Allen.

Among those who participated in the June 26th, 1975, commemoration event at the Grand Opera House besides Donald Criss were renowned trumpet player Marcus Belgrave (who also recorded with Ray Charles, Percy Mayfield, and Doc Cheatham, to name a few) as well as Charles Bowen and James Dixon. All were Boysie Lowery students.

The list of Boysie's students who have performed and recorded jazz—or still do—includes Larry Williams, who has provided invaluable information for this history, Larry's brother Robert, Tony Smith, Larry Unthank, Gerald Chavis, Sly Smithers, Earl Brown, Desmond Kahn, Farid Majeed, Atiba, George Bungy, John

Coley, Earl Simpkins, and, by no means least, Maurice Sims. There are most likely many more about whom we have no knowledge.

Boysie Lowery's influence, whether as a teacher or as a mentor, has been essential in keeping the jazz spirit alive in Wilmington from the late 40s through to today, but especially in the period after the tragedies and turbulence of the 1960s, and even after Wilmington jazz clubs had to close their doors. The spirit of local jazz nurtured by Boysie Lowery led to new efforts to create places where jazz could be heard by the area's astute jazz audience. One of the places, the aforementioned Flight Deck, survived by locating in a more or less central location in New Castle County, easily accessible to those in the city and from other locations.

The sophisticated sensibilities of jazz lovers, engendered by our long jazz history and by Boysie's imprint, enabled the Flight Deck to draw some top-shelf artists to the area. Here's one example of those who came to play in 1979:

> January 28th, 1979 — Al Grey & Jimmy Forrest
> March 25th, 1979 — Tony Williams
> April 29th, 1979 — Philly Joe Jones
> May 6th, 1979 — Richard "Groove" Holmes
> May 27th, 1979 — Jimmy McGriff

June 21st, 1979 — Al Grey
July 19th, 1979 — Richie Cole
July 26th, 1970 — David "Fathead" Newman
August 30th, 1979 — Jimmy Smith
September 2nd, 1979 — Art Blakey
September 29th, 1979 — Hank Crawford

The move of the Flight Deck to 5th and Market Streets in Wilmington did not prove successful, the club having to close in 1983. Experiments to revive life in Wilmington, like turning Market Street into a pedestrian mall for example, were inadequate for a severely damaged and still traumatized city.

Nonetheless, a couple of jazz clubs opened their doors in the early 1980s and provided venues for the better part of the decade. One of those was the Boardroom at 7th and Tatnall Streets. The other was the Ambrosia at 16th and Claymont Streets in the northeast part of Wilmington, but these and some smaller efforts could not recapture the vibrancy of a bygone era.

Today the spirit of Wilmington jazz continues to prevail. One way is through the Clifford Brown Jazz Festival held every summer on Rodney Square. Local jazz is still performed sporadically at venues like the Nomad near 9th and Orange Streets, or Celebration at 340 South

Market Street, Gallucio's at 1709 Lovering Avenue, or the Christina Cultural Arts Center at 705 North Market Street.

If at dawn you stand in the center of downtown Wilmington and listen real carefully, you can still hear a whole century of jazz from those who played it, and if you listen really hard, you can hear Boysie's horn.

Afterword

by Larry Williams

The 1970s was a relatively bleak period for jazz in Wilmington. The dominant musical genre of the day was Fusion, which was being recorded by jazz musicians with varying degrees of success. Locally, funk music was the way to go if you were a working musician; venues such as the Elk's Home on East 11th Street, the American Legion on 10th and Kirkwood Street, and the Longshoreman's Hall on South Claymont Street in my Southbridge neighborhood catered more to pop and funk than to jazz.

The 1980s brought a return to "real" jazz, to use today's term. Early in the decade, a couple of new venues opened in Wilmington that provided a place for aspiring jazz players to perform. The first club was the Boardroom, located on the corner of 7th and Tatnall Street, where you could hear live jazz seven nights a week, plus some intense Saturday afternoon jam sessions. A good example of what the atmosphere was like comes courtesy of trumpeter Gerald Chavis, who recorded a live set there. The other club, Ambrosia, was opened on 16th and Claymont Street in the northeast section of Wilmington by Henry and Barbara Lee. The setting here was, at first, more upscale. The great blues legend Bobby "Blue" Bland once performed there. Saturday jam sessions were held once a month, hosted by saxophonist Harry Spencer. I was part of the scene at both places, and in 1987 I recorded some of the Ambrosia sessions working with Harry Spencer, Coleman Allen, Tommy Ryan, Earle Brown, and others.

Musicians like Harry Spencer or Lee Howell would assemble groups for specific gigs, and I worked some of those. From 1986 to 1989, I was part of Rudolph Koeller's seven-piece group The Melodics, consisting of Tony Smith on trumpet, Vernon James on alto and soprano sax and flute; myself on tenor and alto sax, flute, and arrangements, Chantal Jackson on vocals and flute, Len Foster on piano, Floyd Shiels on bass and vocals and John Spence on drums. Each August, we would do a gig on a cruise ship out of Baltimore's Inner Harbor, and because I always carried a cassette player, much of what we played can be heard today. Another group I was part of in late 1988 was the Basin St. Band, led by trumpeter/trombonist Mario Tollis. Dean Jenkins was the pianist, Val Dobson played bass, with George Wilkerson, Greg Adams, or Jackie Browne on drums. This group worked mainly at two spots in Chester, PA: Norman's Blue Room, on the corner of 3rd & Kerlin St. (no longer there), and the Gold Room on 5th & Edgemont Street, across the street from Cafe Andre, home base for Infinity/Keepers Of The Flame. On many occasions, Millie Cannon and Coleman Allen performed with the band, and much of that music was recorded on cassette.

Around this time, the city of Wilmington began to present live jazz in concert in Rodney Square. It was first known as Jazzin' On The Square, and many of the local musicians contributed to its success. The festival was renamed for Clifford Brown after the surviving members of the Clifford Brown-Max Roach Quintet, with vocalist Helen Merrill, performed here in 1992. The festival continues to this day, though with much less emphasis on Brownie's brand of jazz.

In January 1991, Vernon James assembled a big band to play at a testimonial dinner/dance honoring Robert "Boysie" Lowery. On Sunday,

February 24th, 1991, the event took place at the Brandywine Terrace, 3416 Philadelphia Pike (this venue no longer exists). From this concert, the Boysie Lowery Big Band was born. The first band consisted of Gerald Chavis, Sly Smithers, James Dixon, Greg Davis (Trumpet), Nate Davenport, Darryl Payton, Greg Robinson (Trombone), Vernon James (Alto/Soprano Sax), Harry Spencer (Alto Sax), Lee Howell (Tenor Sax), Larry Williams (Tenor Sax/Flute), Trevor Speck (Baritone Sax), George Bungy (Keyboards), Joe Kearney (Bass), Stan Williams (Drums) plus Dexter Koonce (Guitar), Fostina Dixon-Kilgoe (Soprano Sax) and John Coley (Drums). Also featured were Alfie Moss and Larry Unthank. The concert was a success, and thanks to Keith Smith engineering the sound, I got a recording of it.

    The Boysie Lowery Big Band had a five and one-half-year run (1991-1996). Vernon was band director in the beginning, and that role passed on to me. Other notable musicians who were part of the band were Farid Majeed on trumpet, Earl Simpkins and Ray Calloway on trombones, Earle Brown and Larry Unthank on saxophone, Pete McCarthy on bass, A.J. Malme on drums, Atiba on percussion, Roosevelt "Daahoud" Wardell, Stan Carter, and George Bungy on piano, and the wonderful Sylvia Jackson on vocals.

In addition to many taped rehearsals, some live sets were recorded on cassette, CD, and DVD, plus a studio recording done at the Christina Cultural Arts Center on March 19th, 1994. The band broke up shortly before Boysie's death in early September 1996.

Haneef's African Festival was another popular event during the summer in the mid-1990s. Held for most of its life at Kirkwood Park behind Stubbs School before moving to Brandywine Park in 1996, it was the scene of a lot of great local jazz. I played many concerts in the park with bands and combos including the Boysie Lowery Big Band and Roosevelt Wardell's Artet, with Tony Smith, Vernon James, Wayne Morgan, Kenyatta, and Brandi Cooke. The Big Band and the Artet were also captured on tape.

The 21st century has added to the ghosts of yesterday. Many of the venues I mentioned earlier have disappeared, victims of progress. Even sadder, many of those who were the soul of Wilmington jazz have departed: Millie Cannon, George Wilkerson, Vernon James, Larry Unthank, my brother Robert Williams, George Bungy, Earl Simpkins, Roosevelt Wardell, Dean Jenkins, Lee Howell, Harry Spencer, Coleman Allen, Boysie Lowery, Wilby Fletcher. But I still hear the echoes of their spirits, and in our group Keepers Of The Flame (formerly Infinity), we try to channel those spirits in our music. A special shoutout to two other gentlemen: Richard Blackwell, for the role he played in helping to, in his words, keep this music alive, and Maurice Sims, who connects the past to the present.

My apologies for going on so long but doing this is kind of like playing a solo. If the groove is right, you don't count bars, you just let it flow. That's what I've done here. I'm blessed to have been a part of Wilmington's jazz history, and my hope is that the reader will feel that sense of history and hear Boysie's horn.

Index

Symbols

12 Clouds of Joy 10
2000 Years ii

A

ABC Paramount 34
Adams, Greg 89
Adderley, Cannonball 36
A Found Cacophony 14
Afternoon Detective Agency, The ii
Al Cato Quintette 52
Allen, Coleman 9, 42, 50, 83, 88, 89, 91
Allen, Marian 28, 32, 38, 53
Allen, Sylvester (Papa Dee) 57
Allied Kidd tannery 6
Amazing Stories 7
Ambrosia 85, 88
American Legion 87
Anderson, Ken 2
Andrews, Harry 13
Andy Kirk and his 12 Clouds of Joy 10
Animals 72
"Another Opus" 66
Another Opus 66
Apollo Theater 25
Arden Guild Hall 34
Argo label 36
Arnold, Dave 34
Artet, The 91
Artie Wells Band 6, 10, 42, 83
Atiba 77, 83, 90
Attic, The 72

August Quarterly 64
AUMP Church 64
Austin, Jane 24

B

Baker, Chet 20
Bali Hai 61, 68, 75
Bancroft 4
Banks, Danny 18
Basin St. Band 89
Basin Street 19, 20
Beehive 20
Belgrave, Marcus 77, 83
Belle, Queen 10, 81
Bell's Funeral Home 71
Benjamin, Joe 18
Benny Goodman Band 36
Berklee College of Music 81
Berkowitz, Jerry 72
Berton, Bob 15
Best Is Yet to Come, The 77
Best of Max Roach and Clifford Brown in Concert, The 18
Bethlehem label 30
Betts, Ketter 18
Big Band, The 91
Big Maybelle 36
Billboard chart 67
Bill Haley and the Comets 67
Bill's Café 8
Birdland 17
Birmingham Jazz Festival 66
Black, Brown & Beige Suite 7
Blackwell, Richard 92
Blakey, Art 17, 85
Bland, Bobby "Blue" 88

Bledsoe, George 18
Blue Flames 15, 46
Blue Note 17, 30
"Bluesology" 66
"Blues Prayer" 66
Boots and His Buddies 10
Boptime 106
"Both Barrels" 66
Bowen, Charles 77, 83
Boyd Raeburn Band 31
Boysie Lowery Big Band 90, 91
Brandywine Music Box 33
Brandywine Park 91
Brandywine Terrace 90
Breath and Glamour ii
Brown, Bill 65
Brown, Clifford 2, 3, 10, 11, 13, 14, 15, 16, 18, 19, 22, 23, 25, 26, 29, 30, 32, 33, 37, 44, 45, 46, 69, 70, 71, 73, 77, 78, 80, 85, 89
Brown, Earle 88, 90
Brown, Felix 9
Brown, LaRue 19
Brown and Roach, Incorporated 18
Browne, Jackie 89
Brownie Speaks 14
Brubeck, Dave 20, 36
Bryant, Willie 10
Willie Bryant and His Orchestra 10
Bungy, George 90
Burdon, Eric 72
Burton, Bobby 13, 30
Burton, William (Dutch) 55
Burton's Tonsorial Parlor 8

C

"Cabaret Night with Don Elliot Versatile Jazz Artist of TV Recording Fame and His Quartet" 34
Café Continental 25
Calloway, Cab 10
Calloway, Ray 90
"Canadian Sunset" 67
Candi label 74
Caney's Tailor Shop 6
Cannon, Millie 25, 31, 32, 51, 52, 68, 75, 80, 89, 91
Carnegie Hall 7, 19
Carter, Stan 90
Catalano, Nick 14
Cato, Al 52
Cats and the Fiddle 67
Caulk, Austin O. 24
Cazz, Lou (Lou Casapulla) 74
Cecil Scott and His Bright Boys 10
Celebration 85
Charley Robinson's Jazz Men 31
Chavis, Gerald 59, 83, 88, 90
Chavis, James J. 74
Chavis label 74
Chippey, Willard Burns 5, 39
Chocolate Dandies 12, 40
Chowning, John 34
Chris Powell and his Blue Flames 15
Christina Cultural Arts Center 86, 91
Circle Bar 8, 30
City of Ghosts, A ii
Claude and Artie Wells Band 6, 10, 83
Clifford Brown and Max Roach at

Basin Street 20
Clifford Brown Jazz Festival 85
Clifford Brown/Max Roach Quintet 18, 45
Clifford Brown Memorial Scholarship Fund 33
Clifford Brown, The Life and Art of the Legendary Jazz Trumpeter 14
Clifford Brown Walk 29
Clifford Brown with Strings 19
Club Baby Grand 9, 20, 30, 32, 35, 43, 46, 48, 55, 61, 65, 66, 67, 69, 72, 73, 75
Club Harlem 8, 9, 15, 32, 42, 43
Clyde, James "Red" 13, 30
Cole, Richie 58, 76, 85
Coley, John 83, 90
Collegiates, The 34
Crazy Chris Colombo 66
Colt .38 police revolver 71
Consolidated Artists Production 66
Continental Restaurant 20
Continettes, The 74
Cook, Robert 70
Cooke, Brandi 91
Cordrey, Bob 13, 30, 32, 63
Cotton Club (Cleveland) 20
Crescendo (Camden, NJ club) 18, 72
Crescendo label 18
Criss, Donald (Rashid Yaya) 13, 30, 77, 83
Crosby, Bing 7

D

Dameron, Tadd 15
Davenport, Nate 59, 90
Davidson, Scott 1, 28, 38, 43, 45, 46, 48, 49, 50, 51, 52, 57
Davis, Ardell (AKA Lem Winchester) 22
Davis, Billy 57, 60, 83
Davis, Gregory 59
Davis, Joe 32, 49
Davis, Lemuel Sewell "Ardel" (AKA Lem Winchester) 22
Davis, Marion 22
Davis, Sammy, Jr. 76
Definitive Black & Blue Sessions, The 76
DeKoenigswarter, Baroness Kathleen 37
"Delaware Coon" 6
Delaware Historical Society 2, 39
"Delaware Jazz Workshop's Cabaret Night" 35
Delaware Spectator 2, 3, 105
Delaware Star 3, 105
Delaware State College 14, 25
Delaware State News, The 106
Delaware Valley Star, The 105
Deuces of Rhythm 7, 9, 10, 13, 43
Dick Kenny Quartet 33
Dixon, James 59, 77, 83, 90
Dixon-Kilgoe, Fostina 90
DJ Spooky 82
Dobson, Val 89
Dockery, Sam 19
Dollar Bill's Grotto 6
Dolphy, Eric 17
Donaldson, Bobby 19

Donaldson, Lou 15, 17, 33
Downbeat 33
"Down Fuzz" 61
Dreamstreets 14, 106
"Dude, The" 61
Duke Ellington Orchestra 36
Dunbar, Alice 4
Dunbar, Paul Laurence 4
Dunleith School 61
duPonts 4
Durham, Bobby 76
Duvivier, George 67, 68

E

Eagle Restaurant 62, 63
Eastside 4, 6, 7, 8, 9, 11, 23, 62, 63, 64, 72, 73, 74
Edgehill, Arthur 67
Edwards, Teddy 18
Elk's Home 87
Ellegood's Garage 26
Ellington, Duke 7, 36, 41
Elliott, Bill 67
Elliott, Don 34, 35, 36
EmArcy label 18
Erskine, Bill 69
Estell, Oscar 16

F

Farmer, Art 16
Feather, Leonard 36
Ferguson, Maynard 18, 36
Fiore, Nick 66
Fisher, Rebecca L. 1
Flanagan, Tommy 20, 61
Fleming, Bob 2
Fletcher, Wilby 59, 82, 91
Ford, Dee Dee 67

Forrest, Jimmy 67, 84
Foster, Len 32, 61, 82, 88
Freeman, Russ 17
Friends School 7
fun time house 6, 7

G

"Gala Evening" 68
Galbraith, Barry 18, 19
Gallucio's 86
Gardner, Don 67
Gaye, Marvin 81
Geller, Herb 18
George's Café 9
Gillespie, Dizzy 14
GNP Crescendo label 18
Golson, Benny 16, 61
Goodman, Benny 36
Goomplotz ii
Gordon, Bob 17
Grand Prees 74
Great Depression 8, 12
Grimes, Lloyd "Tiny" 67
Gryce, George General "Gigi," Jr. 16

H

Haley, Bill 67
Hampton, Lionel 16, 24, 31
Haneef's African Festival 91
Hanson, Jessie McCoy 5
Harlem Renaissance 5, 12
Haslan, George 30
Haynes, Roy 18, 65, 67, 68
Heard, J.C. 66
Hearn Brothers 24
Heath, Jimmy 15
Heath, Percy 15, 16

Hefti, Neal 19
Henderson, Fletcher 10
Henry, Herman 35
Hinsley, Jimmy 7, 9
Hinton, Milt 19
Holiday, Billie 67
Holiday Inn 60, 72
Holland, Doug 32, 49, 50
Holloway, Herman, Jr. 3, 105
Holmes, Richard 77
Holt, Isaak "Red" or "Redd" 37
Hope, Elmo 15
Hopkins Theatre 64
Howard High School 5, 11, 12, 13, 23, 24, 25
Howard University 6
Howard University Band 6
Howell, Leander 59
Howell, Lee 88, 90, 91
Hurricane Bar 69

I

"I Come From Jamaica." 15
"Ida Red," 15, 46
Infinity 86, 88, 93. *See also* Keepers Of The Flame

J

Jackson, Al 76
Jackson, Billy 43
Jackson, Chantal 88
Jackson, Milt 66, 77
Jackson, Sylvia 90
Jackson, Mahalia 36
James, Vernon 59, 77, 82, 88, 89, 90, 91

Jane. Joe 15
Jazzin' On The Square 86. *See also* Clifford Brown Jazz Festival
Jazz Venues in Wilmington Area
Ambrosia 85, 88
American Legion 87
Arden Guild Hall 34
Attic, The 72
Bali Hai 61, 68, 75
Bill's Café 8
Brandywine Music Box 33
Brandywine Park 91
Brandywine Terrace 90
Café Continental 25
Celebration 85
Christina Cultural Arts Center 86, 91
Circle Bar 8, 30
Club Baby Grand 9, 20, 30, 32, 35, 43, 46, 48, 55, 61, 65, 66, 67, 69, 72, 73, 75
Club Harlem 8, 9, 15, 32, 42, 43
Daisy Winchester's 6, 7
Dollar Bill's Grotto 6
Dunleith School auditorium 61
Elk's Home 87
Gallucios 86
George's Café 9
Holiday Inn 60, 72
Kilroy's Tavern 62
Kirkwood Park 91
Longshoreman's Hall 87
Marshall's Restaurant 34
Midtown Grill 62
New Castle County Air Base

Enlisted Men's Club 61
Nomad, the 85
Odd Fellows Temple 14
Palace Café 9
Parkway Lounge 33
Roundtable 62, 75
Saint Andrew's School 57
Sans Souci 25, 28, 32, 38, 50, 53, 54, 55, 61, 62, 64, 65, 72, 75, 76
Shriner's auditorium 35
Spot Grille 8, 30, 32, 42, 64
St. Anthony's auditorium 74
Wilmington Armory 68
Wilmington Drama League Theatre 33
Jefferson, Jerome 74
Jenkins, Dean "Deanie" 32, 52, 62, 75, 83, 89, 91
Jes Grew 60, 63
Jim Crow 4, 32, 55, 60, 63
Jimmy Hinsley and His Maniacs of Rhythm 9
Jobe In Exile ii
Jodimars, The 67
Joe Davis Trio 49
Joe Thomas and His Royal Swingsters 9
Johnny & the Dreams 74
Johnson, Gus 66
Johnson, Osie 19
Johnson, Pete 36
Johnson, Preston 25, 30, 31, 45, 49, 50, 54, 72
Johnson, Roy 65
Jones, Eddie 66
Jones, Etta 67
Jones, Hank 66
Jones, Jimmy 18
Jones, Philly Joe 15, 16, 84
Jones, Quincy 16, 19
Jordan, Louis 7, 9, 43
"Joy Spring" 37
J & S Market 24

K

Kansas City 9, 10
Kearney, Joe 59, 77, 90
Keepers Of The Flame 89, 91
Keeys, Justine (Miss Justine) 58, 78
Kenny, Dick 33
Kenyatta 91
"Kids, The" 68
Kilroy's Tavern 62
King, Rev. Dr. Martin Luther 74
King Street Service Center 8
Kirk, Andy 10
Kirkwood Park 91
Klein, Manny 60, 72
Koeller, Rudolph 88
Kogomahalis, Dimitri 2
Korean War 16, 25

L

Land, Harold 17, 18, 19
Last Place on Earth, The ii
Leech, Steven Bio 105
Lem's Beat 65
Levin Waters Confectionery 8
Lewis, Ramsey 37, 60
Lightly and Politely 72
"Like Someone In Love" 66
Lindamood, George 34
Lionel Hampton Band 31
Little Comache 11

Longshoreman Local 1426 26
Longshoreman's Hall 87
Lonnie & the Crisis 74
Loose Walk 77
Louis Jordan's Tympany 5 9
Boysie Lowery iii, v, vi, vii, 7, 13, 14, 37, 43, 44, 59, 73, 74, 77, 78, 79, 80, 81, 82, 83, 84, 86, 89, 90, 91, 92, 94, 99
Lowery, Bud 7, 43
Lytle, Johnny 66, 67

M

Magic City 75
Majeed, Farid 83, 90
Malme, A.J. 90
Mance, Julian Clifford "Junior," Jr. 18, 66
Maniacs of Rhythm 7, 9
Mann, Shelley 17
Manny Klein Trio 60, 72
marijuana 37
Marshall, Wendell 61, 65, 69
Marshall's Restaurant 34
McCarthy, Pete 90
McDuff, Jack 67
McFadden, Eddie 68
McFerrin, Bobby 77
McGriff, Jimmy 67, 84
McLawler, Sarah 67
McShann, Jay 10
Melodics, The 88
Merrill, Helen 18, 89
"Message from Boysie, A" 37
Michelot, Pierre 16
Midtown Grill 62
Milhaud, Darius 12

Miss Elsie's Chicken Shack 8
Miss Justine 58, 78
Modernists 33, 34, 35, 57, 60, 61, 65, 69, 70, 72, 77, 80
Mondragon, Joe 17
Monk, Thelonious 37, 38
"Moodsville" 68
Moore, Sharon 25
Morgan, Wayne 91
Morris, Henry "Peck" 2, 6, 9, 10, 30, 40, 63
Morris, Ralph 2, 3, 14, 30, 45, 55, 56, 63, 105
Morris, Vaughn 3
Morrow, George 17, 18
Mosley, Don 76
Mother African Union Church 5
Mount Joy Methodist Church 71
Mount Zion Cemetery 71
Mr. Horse Collar 43
Mulligan, Gerry 20, 36
Mullins, Herb 16
"Mysticism" 61

N

NAACP 68
Na's Beauty Shoppe 8
National Theater 8, 64
Native Son 24
Nazism 12
Nelson, Benny 76
Nelson, Oliver 65, 67
Neves, John 36
New Castle County Air Base Enlisted Men's Club 61
New Castle County Airport

35, 79
New Faces at Newport 1958 37
New Jazz label 61
New Orleans 9, 10
Newport Jazz Festival 20, 36, 72
Nocturne 67
Nomad 85
"Now's the Time" 36

O

Odd Fellows Temple 14
"Once In A While" 17
"Ornithology" 13, 78
Otto, Richard 67
Out & About 106

P

Pacific Jazz label 17
Palace Café 9
Parker, Charlie 10, 13, 15, 36, 70, 78
Parlophone 12
Pathé 12
Paul F. Thompson's Dixieland Band 39
Payton, Darryl 59, 90
Peagler, Curtis 65
Peck & the Radio Boys 6
Pep Bar 15
Perkins, Carl 17, 18
Pettiford, Oscar 19
Peyton, Crash 7, 10
Philadelphia Inquirer, The 106
Philadelphia Tribune. See also *Wilmington Herald Times*
Pieces of a Dream 76

PK Motors 24
Poe's Daughter, Pym's Soul ii
"Polkadots and Moonbeams" 36
Polydor 12
"Portrait of Jenny," 19
Powell, Bud 17
Powell, Chris 15, 46
Powell, Richie 17, 18, 19
Powmia Among the Dragonflies ii
Prestige studios 66
Preston Johnson's Mood Mixers 31
Price, Gerald "Junie" 32, 33, 34, 57, 58, 60, 69, 70, 73, 79, 80, 83
Pride and Prejudice 24
Prohibition 6
Pyne, Joe 56, 63

Q

Quinichette, Paul 18

R

Ra, Sun 75
Radio Boys 2, 6, 10, 30, 40
Raeburn, Boyd 31
Rago, Vinnie 74
Ramsey Lewis Trio 37, 60
Randolph, Louis 43
Raw Suck i, ii
RCA (label) 34
Redding brothers 5
Redding, J. Saunders 5, 6
Redding, Louis L. 5, 6, 62
Red Hill Inn 65
Reflections 82

Renaud, Henri 16
Reveille With Beverly 7
Roach, Max 17
Robinson, Charley 31
Robinson, Gregory 59
Roché, Betty 7, 9, 30, 41, 72, 80
Rolling Stones 81
Rollins, Sonny 20
Roosevelt Wardell's Artet 91
Root, Billy 19
Roundtable 62, 75
Rouse, Charlie 37
Royal Swingsters 9, 42
Russell, Curly 17
Ryan, Tommy 88

S

Saint Andrew's School 57
Salvatori, Jim 51, 75
Samuel's Dry Goods 8
"Sandu" 37
Sans Souci 25, 28, 32, 38, 50, 53, 54, 55, 61, 62, 64, 65, 72, 75, 76
Santisi, Ray 36
Sauter's Music Store 23
Savoy Sultans 7, 9, 41
Saxophone Colossus 20
Schwartz, Thornell 66
Scott, Cecil 10
Scott, Shirley 66
Seal, Wilber 9
Secret Life of Tux Munce, The ii
Settles, Danny 50, 57
Severinsen, Doc 81
Sheppard, Clarence 5
Shiels, Floyd 88
Shihab, Sahib 33

Shipp, Matthew 82
Shriner's Auditorium 35
Silver, Horace 17
Simpkins, Earl 84, 90, 91
Sims, Irvin 46
Sims, Maurice 2, 10, 23, 24, 26, 46, 47, 50, 62, 84, 92, 105
Sims, Zoot 17, 76
Smith, Carson 17
Smith, Chick 9, 52
Smith, Jimmy 30, 33, 66, 85
Smith, Johnny "Hammond" 65, 68
Smith, Keith 90
Smith, Mamie 5
Smith, Ron 52, 75
Smith, Tony 83, 88, 91
Smithers, Joe "Sly" 59
Smith & Wesson .38 snubnose 70
"Softly, as in a Morning Sunrise" 66
Something Nice 67
Sonny Rollins Plus Four 20
Soul Sister 66
Soviet Union 35
Spanish flu 5
speakeasies 6. *See also* fun time house
Speck, Trevor 90
Spence, John 88
Spencer, Harry 59, 75, 88, 90, 91
Spencer, Peter 64
Spidels 74
Spot Grille 8, 30, 32, 42, 64
Sputnik 35
St. Anthony's auditorium 74
"Stardust," 19

Staton, Dakota 76
Stickney, Felix 3, 105
Stitt, Sonny (Edward Hammond Boatner, Jr.) 33, 58, 76
Storyville Club 19
Strayhorn, Billy 36
Purcell Street 52, 62, 75
Study in Brown 19
Sulieman, Idress 16

T

Tadd Dameron's Big Ten 15
"Take the 'A' Train" 7, 36
Takin' Care of Business 65
Talk That Talk 68
Tasty 78
Taylor, Arthur 61, 65
Teddy & the Continentals 74
Terry, Clark 18
"Things Are Getting Better" 77
Thomas, Joe 9, 42
Thomas, Michael 48
Thomas, Mitch 10, 28, 30, 35, 48
Thomas Reeder's Restaurant 8
Thompson, Paul F. 5, 6, 39
Tisone, Ace 19
Tollis, Mario 89
Topper Club and Lounge 70
Townsend, Robert 43
Trenton Makes, The World Takes 76
Tribute to Clifford Brown, A 37
Tucker, George 65
Turner, Jimmy 43
Tympany Five 7, 43

U

University of Maryland 14, 25
University of Pennsylvania 12
Unthank, Larry 59, 83, 90, 91
Untime ii
urban renewal 64

V

Valdemar's Corpse ii, 106
Van Gelder, Rudy 20
Vaughan, Sarah 18, 33, 38, 76, 81
Verve label 18
Viale, Jean-Louis 16
Vines, Ziggy 19
violbone 6, 39. *See also* Chippey, Willard Burns
VonRiper, Floyd 45

W

Wade, Ida Mae 15, 46
Walnut Street YMCA 5, 35
WAR 72
Wardell, Roosevelt "Daahoud" 90
Washington, Dinah 18, 33, 38
Washington, Grover, Jr. 77
Waters, Levin 8
Watkins, Doug 20
Watts, Ernie 81
WDEL 9
Wedgehorn Manifesto, The ii
Weill, Kurt 12
Wells, Artie 6, 9, 10, 83
Wells, Claude 6, 9, 10, 83
West Chester University 81
Weston, Randy 37

"Where It Is" 37
Wilkerson, George 32, 89, 91
Wilkerson, Millie. *See also* Cannon, Millie
Williams, Joe 76
Williams, Kelly 72
Williams, Larry 59, 83, 87, 90
Williams, Robert 91
Williams, Stan 52, 75, 90
Williams, Walter 16
Williamson, Stu 17
Willie Bryant and His Orchestra 10
"Willow Weep for Me." 19
WILM 9, 28, 63
Wilmington Armory 68
Wilmington Drama League Theater 33
Wilmington Gazette 3
Wilmington Herald Times 8, 42. See also *Philadelphia Tribune*
Wilmington Morning News, The 35
Wilmington Police Department 24, 25, 26
Wilmington Spectator 3
Wilson, Arthur "Skinny" 26
Wilson, Bop 32
Winchester, Bessie 23, 48
Winchester, Daisy 6, 7, 9, 10, 43
Winchester, Lem 1, 2, 22, 23, 24, 25, 27, 28, 31, 32, 33, 34, 35, 36, 44, 47, 48, 49, 50, 54, 57, 60, 62, 64, 66, 68, 69, 71, 74, 75, 77, 80, 82, 83
Winchester, Lemuel, Jr. 33

Winchester, William J. 23, 24
Winchester Special 61, 82
WIOR 20
With Feeling 68
Wittenberg College 34
Wooding, Sam 12, 13, 23, 25, 40
World War II 9, 13, 30, 32, 43
Wright, Richard 24
WTUX 46
WVUD i, 106
Wyands, Richard 67, 68

Y

Yaya, Rashid 13, 77, 83
"You Do" 78
Young, El Dee 37
You've Got To Go When The Wagon Comes 7

Z

Zappa, Frank 81
Zitano, Jimmy 36

Biography of Steven Leech

Steven Leech was born in Wilmington. In the mid-1970s, he began writing for *The Delaware Spectator*, published by Ralph Morris, who is considered to be the Dean of Delaware Black Journalism. In 1976, along with Morris and Herman Holloway, Jr., he helped found *The Delaware Star*, the successor to *The Delaware Spectator*, and served as Managing Editor. When *The Delaware Star* became *The Delaware Valley Star*, Wilmington's final weekly newspaper and with new publisher Felix Stickney, Steven Leech became Editor, serving at times in that capacity with Ralph Morris and Maurice Sims.

Steven Leech's articles have appeared in

Out & About magazine and *The Delaware State News*, with op-eds in *The Wilmington News Journal* and *The Philadelphia Inquirer.* Since 1980 he has served as an editor for *Dreamstreets,* a local literary publication and radio program. He has written extensively about the history of Delaware literary art culminating with his book *Valdemar's Corpse.*

Steven Leech is in radio station WVUD's Hall of Fame. From WVUD, the University of Delaware radio station, he regularly broadcasts his radio program *Boptime* and often plays recordings from Wilmington jazz, R&B, and rock n' roll performers from the past.

Steven Leech currently lives in a cramped apartment in suburban New Castle County where he staves off poverty and communes with the ineffably divine spirit dreaming in every living being.

www.ingramcontent.com/pod-product-compliance
Lightning Source LLC
Chambersburg PA
CBHW040554010526
44110CB00054B/2678